Heavenly Addiction

Overcoming Addictions God's Way

David C. Heebner, LLC
14143 Robert Paris Court
Chantilly, Virginia 20151

ISBN: 153057868X
ISBN-13: 978-1530578689

Cover and interior design: Sarah Deutsch
Editor: Sarah Deutsch

Printed in the United States of America

This book is proudly dedicated to all the clients and their families that I had the privilege of working with over the years since my first job as an addiction therapist at White Deer Run in Allenwood, Pennsylvania, way back in 1990. I have learned much more from each of you than I ever thought possible.

Once again, I am so thankful to my family and friends, who continue to put up with my long hours of counseling and writing. I am forever grateful for your wonderful love and support.

Contents

Introduction

"It's Not My Fault"

We did not choose to be born. We did not choose our parents. We did not choose where to live. We did not choose to be born in sin.

I accepted Christ as my Savior at age thirteen. I accepted that Christ died on the cross to set me free from being born into sin. Sadly, I never experienced actually feeling this freedom Christ gave me until about the age of sixty. I stayed in my mental prison for forty-seven years after the day I was officially released. Why? I didn't know any better.

I knew God set me free from my sin, but I never knew he also set me free from my shame. I was taught that shame was a good thing. I was taught that it helped me to commit fewer sins. However, shame only taught me to feel bad and to stay stuck in the bondage of sin that Christ set me free from. I knew in my mind that Christ set me free but I never experienced the feeling of freedom in my heart. I never discovered how to simply walk out of the prison doors that were no longer locked but were wide open inviting me into a new life without being held captive in sin and shame.

I discovered very early in life the feeling of "it's my fault," and I learned quickly how to stay stuck in shame. Like many of my clients, I knew intellectually that I did not choose to be born, or choose my parents, or choose where or how I grew up. Yet, I carried the constant burden of blaming myself for anything and everything that went wrong in my life. There seemed to be no one else to blame but me. I felt the constant, crushing weight of the belief that "it's my fault."

It never occurred to me, until after forty-seven years of accepting that Christ died on the cross for me, that his crucifixion was an invitation to carry that weight for me. What an experience to feel that weight lifted from me!

While employed at an alcohol and drug residential treatment center, I saw firsthand the clients who carried such a heavy weight of shame on their backs. To assist these clients in their recognition of this heavy load, our staff would have them carry a bag of rocks slung over their shoulder. The rocks would vary in size, with the biggest rock representing the subject matter of their deepest shame. As these clients opened up and shared in group therapy sessions about their shame, they would actually experience the weight being lifted off their backs as we took the rocks out of their bags.

I pray that this book will show each of you how to experience the feeling of freedom that follows this same release of shame, hopefully at a much younger age than I was when I experienced my own release. In your life, I pray that the knowledge of God's love and the experience of his love will merge together for you as you continue to read.

I also specifically pray that our church and counseling leaders be released from shame. I pray that this book does not cause any additional shame for these leaders. I recently caught myself feeling some shame because my transformation did not begin at a much younger age, especially since I have been a Christian counselor for a long time and have held church leadership positions in the past. Throughout the pages of this book, I will frequently identify both our culture and our churches as the culprits in not teaching how we experience a shame-free, intimate, loving relationship with Christ. However, I am only pointing out this truth to invite leaders and followers alike to discover what Christ has to offer us. I am the chief of culprits; even though at my age, I am older and should be wiser than almost any leader I pick on.

There is a church leader who, for more than fourteen years, has shared similar ideas about shame. James Alison, in his book, "Jesus the Forgiving Victim" writes about this subject matter in "Essay Five—On receiving the gift of faith." Alison writes that the normal human framework for the use of words like faith and belief "is one of relaxation, and yet when those words turn 'religious' they suddenly lose that, and appear to become demands for something which inspired the exact reverse of relaxation" (Alison, 2013, 189).

I distinctly recall sitting in a church service about ten years ago where the pastor chastised all of us sitting in the pews for not having enough faith to keep a woman alive who had just died the night before after a long ordeal with cancer. I felt tons of shame and I had never even met the woman. Alison writes in the same essay that the type of faith this pastor was talking about in the church service was a "so-called 'faith' that becomes a very stressful matter, something that you have to work at, and even feel. Something which you are constantly on the verge of losing. Something very demanding" (Alison, 2013,188).

Faith is not something to achieve by thinking our way into a positive state of mind. Alison describes faith as "the habitual disposition which knows and trusts the regular certainty of what is about us, without any need to see it or think about it at all" (Alison, 2013, 191). As it fits in with how God designed our brain, faith is sensory and dwells on that side of the brain, not the thinking side. God created faith as a gift to connect us to him because God did not design us to be able to have faith in ourselves or each other. We are unreliable when it comes to running our own lives or the lives of others.

Alison says it this way: "We are inducted into a world in which we are typically in rivalry with each other, take revenge upon each other, need to despise some people, conceive of our security and well-being as something which depends on others being excluded from it, mislead and abuse each other. However, perhaps even more important than this sort of dangerousness is the accidental, non-deliberate dangerousness by which we affect each other greatly" (Alison, 2013,193-4).

We need to receive the gift of faith in God *from God* because we are unreliable, both in dealing with ourselves and with others. God did not make us to be self-reliant. No wonder we so naturally and automatically blame ourselves for screwing up! We all inherited a self-identity of being screw-ups. Only God can rescue us from this self-identity and its close companion, self-blame, where we continually feel everything is our fault.

God sent Christ to live on this earth and then to be crucified as his rescue mission to save us from our self-condemning destiny. There was no other way to release us from our inherited "It's My Fault" mental state than for Christ himself to carry the blame for all our past, present and future screw-ups. Christ took everyone's blame on himself to release us from our self-conceived notion that everything is our fault.

Christ's death took away any reason to blame ourselves by inviting us to run to him when we experience even a twinge of shame. He wants us to give our shame to him so we can be released from any reason to self-focus and to give us every reason to focus on him.

I have totally given up on myself to ever be able to fight off and overcome my own self-incrimination. Thankfully, God has set me free from any expectation that I should be able to be an overcomer. God is the overcomer. God can absorb my shame without blinking. There is nothing I could ever do, say, think, or feel that could cause God to push me away from his love. I have learned down through the years that I am highly capable of screwing up anything and everything. Thank God for his unconditional love!

What I never knew before was that God did not create me with the expectation that I could overcome the sinful self that I was born with. He also never expected me to be able to overcome my shame either. I was born with the shame, too. I simply do what all my ancestors have always done. This is why God sent Christ to be crucified. This was God's only way to show us how to escape our own sin and shame. He did for us what we are incapable of doing for ourselves.

What stands in the way of us receiving God's gift of salvation without any strings attached? What blocks us from making the simple choice to receive this gift is our inherited ignorance of how to accept unconditional love. Despite God's clear description in his Word of his plan of salvation, our ancestors have altered this plan down through the years. This alteration boils down to mankind's insistence that there must be something we have to do to deserve this gift. Since the original sin by Adam and Eve, there has been nothing mankind could do to earn their freedom from sin and shame. Christ's death on the cross was the only way for us to receive absolution. Our only part is to accept this gift. I have spent most of my lifetime not knowing how to accept God's gift. I am grateful that I have been led out of my ignorance. I now experience this acceptance through my sensory focus on God. This acceptance and focus is a simple choice that requires no effort or sacrifice on my part, just a simple, ongoing choice to experience God through my five senses on a forever basis.

In this world of human relationships, our culture and church are forever coaxing and chiding people to stand up and accept accountability for their actions. In other words, we are taught to accept responsibility for our screw-ups. We are taught to take ownership of our problems and take action to fix these problems. Our culture and church (of which I have been the chief culprit over the years) have been telling and expecting everyone to do something they are constitutionally incapable of doing. Yes, I will say it directly, we are incapable of change; unless, of course, it is for the worse. I do not say this to discourage anyone. I say this hoping all of us will accept the freedom God gives us from trying to fix ourselves.

There is only one source of change. It is not the power of positive thinking or cognitive behavioral therapy. The only source of change is God, and the only change worth trusting is God-induced change. The beautiful thing about God-induced change, according to Alison, is that God moves from within, changing us without displacing us (Alison, 2013). He created us and in no way ever wants to get rid of us. He simply wants to protect us from ourselves and our inherited inability to do anything good.

How does God accomplish this work in us? In order to answer this very important question, we need to address what it means to have faith in God. As with everything else in life, our culture and church teach us that the faith factor is on us, that the amount of faith we produce is what makes all the difference in our relationship with God. This man-made teaching is a direct contradiction to God's real teaching about faith. The accurate equation for the relationship between faith and God is, according to Alison, "One of the things that Jesus was about was that he was creating faith. He was doing something so that we could believe. Effectively, he was saying 'I know that you are susceptible. I know that you find it difficult to believe that God loves you. I know that you are inclined to be frightened of death . . . and [I know] that you are being held in being by someone who is utterly trustworthy. All this I know. What I want to do is to try to nudge you into being able to trust that the one who brought you into being is actually trustable, not out to get you . . . I am going to act out in such a way to make it possible for you to believe—I am setting out to prove God's trustworthiness for you'" (Alison, 2013, 207-8).

Alison continued his writing on the accurate equation between faith and God by saying: "I hope you see that this shifts the whole burden of faith. Rather than an imperious demand that you should try to believe seventeen impossible things before breakfast, this is a picture of someone desperately trying to get across to you that they are trustable. They are not making a demand on us, so much as doing the work so as to induce us into relaxing. And this is central to what I've been talking about all along. The whole burden of faith is on the person who is trying to get you to relax, not on you! Faith is a disposition in you which someone else has worked hard to produce. A disposition in you which someone else has worked to produce is a gift in you from the person who did the work of producing it. This is a complete reversal of the way in which we are accustomed to hearing such things presented" (Alison, 2013, 211-212).

This book you are about to read on "Heavenly Addiction" is also a complete reversal on the way you are used to reading about God and his work in us. This book is about *how* God created us and designed our brains so he could accomplish his work of producing faith in us. This book is about *how* God made us so he could accomplish his work of inducing us into relaxation in him. Earthly addictions are man-made attempts to relax. Heavenly addiction is God's way of producing faith in us to guide us over time to become more and more relaxed in him. The only thing God ever asks of us is to simply choose to place our sensory focus on him. The book is about what sensory focus looks like and how we can activate and elevate the attention of our five senses on God. Yes, this choice becomes habit-forming and addictive—in a good way. God amplifies our desire to watch him more and more as he produces faith in him and guides us into relaxation in all situations in our lives, in both the good times and the bad.

Chapter One

Performance and Beyond

"...How did your new life begin? Was it by working your heads off to please him? Or was it by responding to God's Message to you? For only crazy people think they could complete by their own efforts what was begun by God."

- Galatians 3:2-3, *The Message*

We live in a modern-day culture of ultra-performance expectations. We have gone way beyond normal performance to high-octane, super-charged performance with no end in sight. In the world of work, school, athletics, home, family and church, we have been programed to always be striving to reach a higher level.

However, while our effort-based, turbo-charged, goal-driven, mentally-achieving society may seem like a recent phenomenon, scholastic observations about this trend go back centuries. Over sixty-five years ago, A.W. Tozer, an American preacher, author, and magazine editor who received two honorary doctorate degrees also addressed this subject matter in his best-selling book, *The Pursuit of God.*

Tozer began his book by describing his experience of living in an "hour of all but universal darkness" (Tozer, 2014, 7). He wrote that the church culture of his day needed "a blessed relief from sterile legalism and unavailing self-effort" (Tozer, 2014, 12).

Tozer lamented that this religious culture made the "transaction of religious conversion mechanical and spiritless . . . without creating any special love for [God] in the soul of the receiver" (Tozer, 2014, 12). Tozer also described the church culture of his day as existing in an age of "religious complexity" where "the simplicity which is in Christ is rarely found among us. In its stead are programs, methods, organizations, and a world of nervous activities which occupy time and attention but can never satisfy the longing of the heart" (Tozer, 2014, 15).

Tozer said the church culture of his day was "snared in the coils of a spurious logic which insists that if we have found [God] we need no more seek him. This is set before us as the last word in orthodoxy, and it is taken for granted that no Bible-taught Christian ever believed otherwise. Thus the whole testimony of the worshipping, seeking, singing Church on that subject is crisply set aside" (Tozer, 2014, 14). Tozer desired that the church of his day return to a life like that of David in the Bible, which he describes as "a torrent of spiritual desire" or that of Paul, who "confessed the mainspring of his life to be his burning desire after Christ" (Tozer, 2014,14). Tozer wished fervently that the people of his day would "want to taste, to touch with their hearts, to see with their inner eyes the wonder that is God" (Tozer, 2014, 14).

As Tozer discovered, many people are driven by self-focus and mental effort, yet feel empty inside. Unfortunately, hardly anyone followed up or built upon Tozer's message. Most church and counseling experts in our current culture work day after day with people suffering from performance burnout and living in darkness, yet these same counselors continue to emphasize additional steps of human effort as the way to overcome burnout with an even higher level of performance. In *The Pursuit of God*, even Tozer himself primarily used performance words (like "must") in his instructions to his readers on what they should do to achieve a "mighty longing after God" (Tozer, 2014, 15). For example, Tozer said, "We must simplify our approach to him . . . we must strip down to essentials . . . we must put away all effort to impress" (Tozer, 2014, 15). In his writing, Tozer had the right idea, but missed the mark in the language he chose to use. In much the same way, many church leaders and counseling experts today still miss the mark when they say that we must *put more effort* into putting away an effort-based relationship with God.

This "performance and beyond" treadmill seems to be inherent in all of us as we automatically strive to achieve at higher and higher levels. For a while, the more we run on this treadmill, the more we seem to thrive on it. The more we thrive on it, the more performance permeates every fiber of our daily living. We get up to go to work to perform. We leave work to perform at the gym. We come home from the gym to perform at home with our spouse and family. On a regular basis, we go out socially to perform, and on Sundays, many of us even go to church to perform.

Even when we pause to examine our hearts and feel the desire to draw close to God and our spouse and children, we seem preconditioned to attempt to use our own mental effort to soften our hearts. These attempts are futile and exhausting. The reality is that, by definition, increased mental self-effort only increases our hardness of heart and results in utter frustration and failure. So many suffering people who stay on this self-effort treadmill consistently feel frustrated because they continually try to *think* their way into *feeling* good, yet end up feeling more depressed and hopeless than ever.

In our current performance-driven society where we are expected by ourselves and others to perform at lightning speed, our brains also grow accustomed to racing thoughts and rapid thinking. Our brains start to believe that racing thoughts are a normal part of our everyday lifestyle. Our brain is a creature of habit and can become addicted to these hyper thought-waves. The brain tricks itself into believing that it can race all day and well into the night. Even activities designed for rest and relaxation can easily become part of a performance addiction in our frenetic minds.

Neuroscientists have discovered that God did not design mankind with a thinking brain to constantly run in overdrive. In fact, a racing mind can become dangerous to our health. Our thinking brain has to compensate for running in overdrive at some point and tends to self-correct by applying the brakes and shifting into a much lower gear, frequently causing depression. It is very easy in our current day living conditions to alternate between driving our brain too fast and having it switch to under-drive. This manic-depressive condition constitutes what is categorized in clinical terms as a bi-polar response. The brain overdoses in the fast lane and pulls over and withdraws into the slow lane of depressive thinking. This can occur even in people who do not have a clinical diagnosis of bipolar disorder.

Without being taught how God created our brain with an alternative sensory highway, performance-driven addicts cross back and forth between the slow and fast lanes of the thinking highway. They speed in the fast lane until their "thought engine" gets over-heated and then they struggle and sputter along in the slow lane. They alternate between these manic and depressive speeds of performance out of ignorance, because no one has ever taught them how

God designed our brain to function. They are not even aware that our brain has an alternate, sensory-brain highway that is separate and distinct from the thinking-brain highway, let alone how to switch highways.

God designed our brain with two adjacent centers, each with its own specialization. One center specializes in sensing and the other specializes in thinking. Each center is essentially equal in size, giving the brain a fifty-percent capacity to relax through sensory channels and a fifty-percent capacity to think and work. These two brain centers, each with their own highway, have well-built bridges between them to switch highways. However, despite how God constructed our brains with this incredible design, we have been programmed culturally and religiously to operate and drive on the work-and-effort highway except when we sleep. That means we spend every waking hour in work and effort mode on our thinking highway. As our day progresses, our thoughts naturally keep speeding up, and we drive faster and faster on the thinking highway to try to accomplish everything we are expected to get done for the day. We wake up with our mind pre-programed to immediately start out thinking intensely about what has to get done today. One client told me that he suffers from mental to-do lists that instantly start spinning when he first wakes up in the morning.

The problem with our performance-driven brain is that it starts to get tired and worn out as the day progresses. Since we have been programmed to try even harder to compensate for feeling tired, our brain is tricked into thinking it can keep going on an empty energy tank. Our brain taps into a reserve tank that contains chemicals that act much like cocaine in our body. This artificial stimulant causes our thinking mind to travel faster and faster the more tired we get. We end up feeling so hyped up and cannot fall asleep even though we are exhausted. Our daily existence erodes into an unbalanced mixture of 70-80% nonstop mental racing on our thinking highway and then practically running off the side of the road longing to sleep but sitting there in our car with our eyes wide open unable to fall asleep.

With no brain ability left to be able to rest, our brain loses its God-designed desire to relax. So many of us start our day with a shower and coffee, but do not even allow our minds to enjoy those sensory activities. We barely remember them because our mind was already at the office, busy working. As a result, the sixteen hours we spend a day in performance mode exhausts our brain. Our brain is so overtired that it has no motivation to play recreational activities, or even to relax by reading a good book. We are also often too overtired to sleep. Despite our brain's desperate need to spend time on the sensory side, it has lost its sense of direction and desire to cross the bridge to the sensory brain. At this point, the human brain is incredibly vulnerable to quick fixes or the many earthly addictions like drugs and alcohol, food, pornography, gambling, a host of online addictions and many others too numerous to mention.

As a result of the perfect storm just described, anxiety and sleep disturbance have become "silent" hidden medical conditions that are guaranteed close companions to thinking in overdrive all the time. They are also the guaranteed natural outcomes of the overall performance epidemic that our culture is suffering from. Alarmingly, anxiety and sleep disturbance have no human cure. Of course, the pharmaceutical companies have all kinds of medication cures to offer for anxiety and sleep disturbance, but these supposed cures just end up resulting in earthly pill addictions. Medication cures are also very prone to causing thinking distortions and prone to disturbing the brain's natural ability to rest and relax.

A classic example of a medication solution for sleep disturbance is the pill, Ambien, which is being passed out by the medical profession like trick-or-treat candy. The trouble with Ambien is that it tricks our brain into believing it is a miracle fix. The first few nights Ambien works like a charm to put us to sleep. However, we quickly build up a tolerance to this medication and need to take more and more to have the same effect. Unfortunately, after a week or two, the increased dose of Ambien begins to cause insomnia rather than sleep. As a result, the supposed medical fix has caused even more sleeplessness and anxiety which can lead to our body and mind wearing out and breaking down much faster than the normal aging cycle.

With the supposed medical solution not being a solid, permanent fix, we naturally turn back to our own performance methods to deal with our excess performance. This is like trying to fix the problem with the problem. Some of us try to convince ourselves that we don't need eight hours of sleep. We decide that we might as well put those extra hours when we can't sleep to productive use. We put ourselves to work in some aspect of our lives, a second job, a household project, or night classes to advance our education, just to name a few performance-based solutions.

When we gain money from our extra job or finish the new addition on our house or earn that higher degree, everyone applauds our super-human efforts to achieve. This positive reinforcement only drives us to perform at an even higher level. At this point, the performance treadmill is no longer a challenge, so we upgrade our performance treadmill to performance "stairs." Next thing you know, we feel the need to graduate to high level performance aerobics and even military-type, boot-camp-level workouts. While intense physical training can be great for our bodies, intense mental training quickly takes us beyond endurance to exhaustion. This mental exhaustion tricks our brains into feeling physically exhausted, leaving us with no motivation to do anything but sit around and stare. At this level of mental performance burnout, when we most need our sensory brain to take over and restore us mentally, emotional and physically, we literally feel unable to get off the couch. We feel totally paralyzed to do anything for sensory restoration.

Eventually, we end up trapped in our own mental prison, where we feel unable to escape the addictions of our thinking brain. We have lost the roadmap to our sensory brain, where we could get rest and relaxation. We are left feeling tortured by our racing thoughts that sound like a loud radio station we can't silence. This mental noise can make us feel like we are cracking up or going crazy. Over my thirty-three years in the counseling profession, clients come to see me every day, begging me to help them get the mental noise out of their heads. This noise won't let them sleep; they experience nausea and diarrhea; they lose their appetite for food; they feel unable to communicate with others; they get panicky and start to feel pressure in their chest and pain in other parts of their body. Some clients feel such mental pain that they admit to self-inflicting physical pain just to get some relief. Clients have confessed to cutting, stabbing, burning and other forms of physical self-torture in their desperate efforts to relieve their mental torment.

For other clients, their thinking addictions and mental prisons result in feeling angry all the time. Rather than inflicting pain on themselves, they inflict pain and torture on others. In their own misery, they try to make others miserable. They are constantly flooded with and dwell on angry thoughts. They end up living in emotional isolation because no one wants to be around them. Anger can become one of the earthly addictions that clients hang onto for dear life. In their anger, they find it impossible to feel close to God or each other. David in the Bible experienced a lot of anger, but he also experienced the many times God rescued him from anger. In Psalm 119:53-54, *The Message* shows that this rescue came in the form of sensory focus on music and singing and the emotional relief God brought to David through song.

Unfortunately, many church leaders and counselors censor people's anger. They censor the sensory. This censorship causes guilt and shame and more anger. God created anger, just like he designed other feelings like fear to be our warning signals or red flares to run to him. An eight-year-old client of mine probably said it best: "God is fine when I get angry. He just doesn't want me to go berserk." God has given us millions of sensory alternatives to melt our anger instead of fueling it. Trying to reason with our anger simply adds kindling to the flames and makes the fire hotter. My eight-year-old client loves to get anger out of his system through kick boxing. That is just one example of heavenly sensory solutions functioning as an alternative to earthly, thought-driven, human solutions.

For the first thirty years of my career, I did what most other church leaders and counselors still do with their clients. I would always try to encourage clients by telling them that they still had plenty of mental intelligence and thought power left for us to figure out their problems together. I told them that I would think hard and wanted them to think harder than ever before and not give up until we found solutions to their life issues. I tried to be their cheerleader to build up their self-confidence. I tried to boost their self-egos by sharing my positive thoughts about them. I hoped that they would internalize my positive thoughts and become positive thinkers themselves. I labeled their negative thinking as thought-distortions and challenged them to correct their erroneous thinking.

Like many secular and Christian counselors are currently doing, I loaded up my clients with positive thinking to replace their negative thoughts. In essence, through my cognitive-based solutions, I was feeding the monster of the already overloaded thinking side of the client's brain. Basically, I was trying to push them to become even more mental-performance-driven. My cognitive techniques were only driving them further into the ground. They were left feeling more self-defeated and experienced additional mental anguish. They figured they were the only ones who were not able to grab onto positive thinking and then assumed they were somehow defective and different from everyone else. My efforts to encourage them with positive thoughts only triggered reminders of how bad they felt. Some clients would even end up feeling crazy and thinking that they must be *really* screwed up mentally.

This counseling technique of loading up clients with positive thoughts to replace their negative ones is well-intended and based on some popular techniques. The Thinking Business is a global training company that specializes in teaching people thinking skills. The Thinking Business offers educational services that are designed to help clients achieve personal and professional growth. The company bases the strategies it teaches on brain research, which demonstrates that neural pathways in the brain create patterns of thought.

> "Once these pathways are created, the thoughts are likely to be repeated. This is because, the repetition of a thought decreases the biochemical resistance to that thought happening again and the connections between two brain cells on the neural pathway become stronger. . . Every time you think a thought, the resistance is reduced therefore increasing the likelihood of you having the thought again. This is how habits are formed. And it is why it is vitally important that you monitor your thinking. If you think negatively, you will build a strong connection of negative thoughts so you will be more likely to keep repeating those negative thoughts. Try to ensure that you are creating positive thoughts and good habits" (The Thinking Business, 2016).

Certainly sounds like a great teaching strategy, but the million-dollar question is: exactly *how* do we ensure that we are creating positive thoughts over time, so there is a strong connection in our brain that builds these positive thoughts into a strong lasting habit? It takes more than just thinking positive thoughts or even voicing them out loud. If we really don't believe what we are thinking or saying anyway, these self-improvement attempts are no more than play-acting and pretending. Our personal efforts don't produce a positive outcome anyway. Quite frankly, we simply end up more burned out than ever in our pressure-packed, performance-driven lifestyle of daily living.

Recently, one client was willing to share vivid feelings of where his negative, self-defeatist thoughts took him. He experienced an early morning dream that triggered a negative thought spree where he was hit with huge waves of toxic thoughts that took him to a "psychological cesspool of my own doing." He said that he found it impossible to talk himself down. He emphasized that positive thoughts and even positive memories only brought on more sadness. He ended up feeling so awful that the thought of not being alive to endure these thoughts was comforting and made him feel peaceful.

In my counseling practice, I no longer over-emphasize positive thinking. When I treat clients with depression, I give them permission to discontinue their performance-based efforts to produce positive thoughts. Plus, I don't remind them of the positive thoughts they "should" be having to replace their negative ones. I encourage them to stop trying to manufacture a positive outlook through hyper-focus on themselves and their own thoughts. This includes trying to figure out their negativity. God did not design our human brain to become positive through personal performance. If we could produce positivity in our lives on our own efforts, we would not need God. Only God can provide us with genuine positive thinking and bring us his joy when we focus our five senses on him. He fills us with his amazing thoughts to replace our own negative ones. That is the only way to ensure that positive thoughts are being created in our brains on an ongoing basis. It is the only way that good habits can be produced to replace the existing negative ones.

God showed me through my own personal experience how he ensures that we can be filled with his joyful thoughts that become new habits to replace our own negative thinking. My own life has been a case study of how our brain can build such a strong connection of negative thoughts that they kept repeating themselves. I struggled with this negativity for most of my life-time. My own performance efforts through positive thinking never corrected the problem, which made me feel more and more self-defeated over the years. However, about four to five years ago I began writing my first book, *Clear my Vision*. After about two or three months of my daily study in *The Message*, God showed me how positive thoughts in his Word rubbed off on me and started forming new thought patterns and habits that would drown out my own negative thinking. I experienced such a welcome relief when I discovered a method that actually worked and transformed me into a new person.

God graciously gives us all a life-long way of escape from our own negativistic thought patterns. In *The Message*, Paul writes in Galatians 5:1 that God indeed gave us this way of escape: "Christ has set us free to live a free life. So take your stand! Never again let anyone put a harness of slavery on you." God emphatically warns us never again to let anyone, whether it be the church, our spouse, or even ourselves, drive us into the ground through an anxious, performance-driven, rule-based life. Many churches, many jobs, many schools, many marriages and many families operate in a rule-driven, effort-based, achievement-oriented atmosphere, where the pressure-packed conditions are obvious every day. In this passage from Galatians 5, verses 2-3, Paul also says that if we put our focus on a "rule-keeping system," we will squander this gift of freedom given to us through Christ's "hard-won" victory when he died on the cross.

Paul goes on to say in this same chapter in that "I suspect you would never intend this, but this is what happens." Whether intentionally or through automatic habit, many singles, couples, parents, children, churches, and cultures have fallen into a repetitive pattern where they are so focused on their own thinking and mental effort that they automatically engage in a lifestyle where they "attempt to live by [their] own religious plans and projects." Paul tells the Galatians that because of these efforts, "you are cut off from Christ, you fall out of grace."

Paul did not make this bold statement to be mean or to threaten that God will punish us. The punishment is self-imposed. We allow others, through our focus on their rules and regulations, to ruin our joy of sensory focus on God. We don't need any help from others to ruin our freedom in Christ; we are masters at setting our own performance expectations so high that we work at self-improvement day and night, even on weekends. Whether driven by others or our own insane performance standards, we free-fall out of the protection of God's grace and lose sight of "something far more interior: faith expressed in love" (*The Message,* Galatians 5:9).

I am writing this book on "Heavenly Addiction" to show how God clearly demonstrates, step by step, to anyone who will listen, how to give him the full attention of our five senses. When we do this, we can be emptied of our own negative thoughts and be filled with his joyful thoughts that become new habits over time. Through this simple, moment-by-moment choice, we can devote the continual attention of our five senses to him—no thinking effort necessary! This book is written to demonstrate how God sets people free to live a new sensory life in him. This book describes exactly how God wants to relieve everyone who seeks him of their mental anguish and release them from their self-imposed, anxiety-driven thought traps and mental performance prisons.

I am devoted, through my writing, to explain to readers a radically new kind of therapy. This innovative Christian counseling model—the first of its kind—works from current neuroscientific and psychological principles and is rooted in God's Word. I have named this clinical method "FocusChoice Therapy." Unlike other current secular and Christian approaches to therapy, which are predominately based on cognitive-behavioral theories of counseling, FocusChoice Therapy is uniquely grounded in God's Word and is founded on the basic premise that clients simply choose to give God their sensory focus while he does all the performing in their lives. Read on, and you will learn exactly what it means to have a sensory relationship with God where we devote the full attention of our five senses to God while he does all the work in our daily lives. He wants us to rest and relax in him while he does all the labor in our everyday living. He never wanted or intended us to be anxiety-ridden. He does not even want any effort-based mental or thought-based assistance from us. He clearly instructs us to give him our total sensory attention and just sit back and enjoy the ride of him running our daily lives.

It is a totally foreign concept in Christian therapy and even our church culture to portray God as not wanting us to think for ourselves. Yet, this concept, which is a fundamental construct in this book and in FocusChoice Therapy, is based on God's divine word. Thinking on our own is highly detrimental to our mental, emotional and physical health. Thinking addiction, just like any other earthly addiction, causes serious anxiety, anger and depression in our everyday lives. Thinking impairs our brain's ability to have fun and enjoy life. Thinking gets in the way of living in the moment and devoting our sensory attention to God.

When we give God the full attention of our sense of smell, sound, sight, taste and touch, God designed our brain so he can pour out his thoughts into the thinking side of our brain and completely transform our thought life. God gives us hopeful, uplifting thoughts to replace our woeful, destructive thinking. God literally reshapes our thinking in that way that inspires us with fresh new feelings and desires.

For many years, our Christian counselors and church leaders have supported our culture's belief in the power of positive thinking. However, anything man-made is completely powerless and useless. All power belongs to God. Through the model of FocusChoice Therapy, this book will highlight the power of God-thinking and emphasize God's ability to make all things brand-new.

"Be alert, be present. I'm about to do something brand-new. It's bursting out! Don't you see it? There it is! I'm making a road through the desert, rivers in the badlands" (Isaiah 43:8-19, *The Message*).

Chapter Two

Anxious, Negativistic Thinking

"So let's keep focused on that goal, those of us who want everything God has for us. If any of you have something else in mind, something less than total commitment, God will clear your blurred vision—you'll see it yet!"

- Philippians 3:15-16, *The Message*

I was inspired to discover a new way of living for myself and others after a client translated a letter to me from a friend of his in South America. What stood out in this letter was the above scripture out of *The Message*. The one phrase "He will clear your vision" jumped off the page to me by about five feet. There was no doubt in my mind that God wanted to show me something. What he showed me radically changed my life and will hopefully change many other lives as well.

I was always clueless that God took the responsibility to clear my vision in life. I always thought that was my job! I always felt like a failure at this job because it seemed I could never see clearly how to live my life through my own efforts and performance. For my entire life, or at least as far back as I can remember, I had been performance-driven. Whether in school, sports, work or family life, I strived to be number one, ahead of anyone else. For many years, I achieved at very high levels at school, sports and work.

Despite excellent results because of my competitive drive to succeed in almost every area of my life, that same competitive drive was a disaster in my family life and brought me to the edge of a high emotional cliff, way past the end of my rope. My competitiveness would result in intense, psychological discussions with myself that lasted way too long, and I would experience cascades of negative thoughts that made me feel terrible. The more I tried to analyze and figure out my thoughts regarding my family life, the more I began to live inside my own mental prison in isolation from my family. For me, too much thinking had become dangerous to my emotional health and the well-being of my family life.

The Message in Psalm 107:10-16 gives an accurate description of the impact of my anxious, negativistic thinking on my mental and emotional health during those many years of my life: "Some of you were locked in a dark cell, cruelly confined behind bars, punished for defying God's Word, for turning your back on the High God's counsel—a hard sentence, and your hearts so heavy, and not a soul in sight to help. Then you called out to God in your desperate condition; he got you out in the nick of time. He led you out of your dark, dark cell, broke open the jail and led you out. So thank God for his marvelous love, for his miracle mercy to the children he loves; he shattered the heavy jailhouse doors, he snapped the prison bars like matchsticks!"

God applied this scripture to my life by showing me that my constant, anxious, negativistic thinking was keeping me locked in a dark prison cell. I was punishing myself and had myself cruelly confined behind these mental prison bars because I was totally focused on my own thoughts, which prevented me from focusing on God's

Word or seeking his counsel for my life. I was so hyper-focused on my own thoughts that I did not give him any of my sensory attention to be able to hear his voice. My heart was so heavy and there seemed to be no soul out there in sight who knew how to help me with this heavy burden.

At the lowest and darkest point of my desperate mental condition, I called out to God and begged him to help me. How quickly he responded, in the nick of time, before I forever turned my back on him! In God's unconditional love and mercy, he did not make me try to find my way out of the jail cell in the dark. God himself led me out; he saved me from myself. In his supernatural strength, God broke open the jail, he shattered the heavy jailhouse doors, and he snapped the prison bars like matchsticks. My powerful God showed me clearly that he had the strength and love to give me a full and complete rescue. He showed me that I can totally depend on his strength and love to run my life on a permanent full-time basis.

During my many years of counseling, I have seen countless others who are locked in the same mental prison where I had confined myself. Our brain becomes over-stimulated and anxious when the thinking side is bombarded with thoughts and the sensory side is not utilized to help us relax and rest. Thinking about our negative thoughts in order to figure out or fix our anxiety only makes us more anxious.

The disease of anxious thinking, which paralyzed me in my personal life, haunts the lives of so many other people throughout the world, reaching epidemic proportions, with no human cure in sight. No one in particular can be blamed for this phenomenon. It has been in process and evolving since time began, when God designed the beautiful Garden of Eden and created Adam and Eve to enjoy his masterpiece. He designed their brains exactly like ours. God wanted Adam and Eve to give him their total sensory attention through focus on him with their five senses while he did their thinking for them.

God set up the Garden of Eden so Adam and Eve never had to think for themselves. All God desired from Adam and Eve was for them to continually live in with moment with him, indulging themselves in the sensational environment he created for them. Instead, Adam and Eve chose to let Satan activate the original sin of self-thinking by shifting from sensory focus on God to self-focus on their own thoughts. Satan set the sin of thinking for ourselves in motion by tempting Eve to ponder his thoughts about the tree of good and evil. In Genesis 3:4-5, "The serpent said to the Woman, 'You won't die. God knows that the moment you eat from that tree, you'll see what's really going on. You'll be just like God, knowing everything, ranging all the way from good to evil'" (*The Message*).

It's almost unbelievable. The original sin was not some fancy earthly addiction, it was the sin of choosing to think for ourselves and being impressed with our own knowledge. *The Message* goes on to say in Genesis 3:6 that "When the Woman saw that the tree looked like good eating and realized what she would get out of it—she'd know everything!—she took and ate the fruit and then gave some to her husband and he ate." Through their simple choices to eat the fruit, Adam and Eve became obsessed with thinking for themselves and wanting to know everything.

Adam and Eve's obsessive self-thinking automatically took their sensory focus off God. They became stuck in their endeavors to know everything through their own mental efforts. Their misuse of God's design for the brain not only resulted in disaster for them, but also set all of humanity on the wrong path for the rest of time. Adam and Eve chose to rely on their own reasoning, which resulted in the birth of that anxious, negativistic thinking that has been passed on to every generation since. Anxious negativity is the guaranteed outcome of choosing to continually think for ourselves.

We can never overcome this anxious negativity on our own, but the good news is that God still offers us the same option he gave to Adam and Eve in the beginning. He offers to take over our thinking for us and enable us to relax in him. Since we possess the same brain design that God gave to Adam and Eve, we can make the simple choice to live in the moment with him by giving him our sensory attention. God wants to break the original curse that causes us to become trapped in thinking for ourselves. When we accept his invitation to be continually be in his presence through sensory focus on him, God can heal our anxiety by offering us a Garden of Eden relationship with him, just like the one he intended for Adam and Eve.

Since the original curse of self-focus was set in motion, people everywhere have been enslaved by their own self-thinking and their fierce determination to run their own lives. Their stubbornness causes them to be completely consumed by their own thinking, oblivious to God's love for them and his offer to run their lives and set them free.

Even after Christ demonstrated the depth of his love and commitment to us through his death on the cross, God's offer has not been embraced by our culture or our church. Most of us recognize Christ's death on the cross as his offer to save us and forgive our sins, but many of us do not embrace his desire to be in continual union with us so he can govern our lives each minute of every day. Our resistance to a daily sensory connection with Christ has had catastrophic results down through the centuries, despite the work of experts attempting to address this issue.

One such expert, Dr. Caroline Leaf, a cognitive neuroscientist specializing in neuropsychology, has researched the mind-brain connection since the early 1980's. Dr. Leaf has published numerous articles in academic journals and consumer magazines, and has been widely interviewed in newspapers, on radio shows, and on television shows about her research and theories. She has lectured to both Christian and secular audiences worldwide, linking scientific principles of the brain to spiritual, intellectual and emotional issues.

In an article titled "Toxic Thoughts," Dr. Leaf suggests that 75% to 95% of the illnesses that plague people in today's world are a direct result of their thought life. She believes that we are living in an epidemic of toxic emotions, and that an uncontrolled thought life full of toxicity can actually make a person sick. Dr. Leaf states that research shows that fear, all on its own, triggers more than fourteen hundred known physical and chemical responses and activates more than thirty known hormones. This "toxic waste generated by toxic thoughts causes the following illnesses: diabetes, cancer, asthma, skin problems and allergies, to name a few." Dr. Leaf concludes by recommending that patients begin to consciously control their thought life in order to detox their brain (Leaf, 2016).

How does a person go about consciously controlling their thought life so they can detox their brain and get rid of their toxic thoughts? Dr. Leaf asserts that people can prevent their thoughts from rampaging through their mind by learning to "engage interactively with every single thought that they have, and to analyze it before they decide either to accept or reject it" (Leaf, 2016). This method reminds me of the instructions of Paul in 2 Corinthians 10:5 that we should engage in "casting down imaginations," and in "bringing into captivity every thought to the obedience of Christ" (King James Bible).

From a personal-effort, performance-driven perspective, these instructions seem to be utterly overwhelming. In light of the fact that we have between forty and seventy *thousand* thoughts a day, how is that even humanly possible? Just thinking about having to go through that kind of mental exercise discourages me. In addition, if my thoughts are already toxic and I try to analyze them, my thinking about my thoughts (also known as meta-thinking) will likely be toxic as well.

Through extensive reading about the Bible and the brain, I have learned that holding every thought captive has nothing to do with personal effort or performance or self-analysis. God does not expect us to perform this radical change in our thought life on our own. If we could, we would not even need God. He performs this thought change in us. *The Message* says in Romans 8:5-8 that, "Those who think they can do it on their own end up obsessed with measuring their own moral muscle but never get around to exercising it in real life. Those who trust God's actions in them find that God's Spirit is in them—living and breathing God! Obsession with self in these matters is a dead end; attention to God leads us out into the open into a spacious, free life. Focusing on self is the opposite of focusing on God. Anyone completely absorbed in self ignores God, ends up thinking more about self than God."

How does God take over our thoughts and lead us out into a spacious, free life? As this scripture in Romans says, God simply needs us to give him our attention. This occurs through sensory focus on him. When God has the attention of our five senses, his thoughts have the freedom to enter our thinking brain. God designed our brain so that every time we think one of his thoughts, the likelihood of our brain having that thought again increases. Having this information about how our brain works helps us to see clearly why God seeks our attention on a continual basis. Otherwise, if we go back to self-focus, we will return to anxious, negativistic thinking, increasing the likelihood of our brain repeating those toxic thoughts instead.

Only God can deliver an uplifting and encouraging thought life. God kept his creation very simple by designing only one way to receive his thoughts. That way is our continual sensory focus on him. He repeatedly says in his word that our effort-based performance for him will not give us access to his thoughts. The Bible says in Ephesians 2:8-9, "God saved you by his grace when you believed. And you can't take credit for this; it is a gift from God. Salvation is not a reward for the good things we have done, so none of us can boast about it" (New Living Translation). God designed every one of us, so he knows that human performance efforts wills always result in drawing attention to ourselves and not him. However, when we show we belong to Christ by devoting our senses to him, "he pours his thoughts into us and makes us cheerful no matter what, we are in prayer all the time, and we thank him in every circumstance" (I Thessalonians 5:18, *The Message*).

With our sensory focus on God, who pours his thoughts into us, what happens to our own anxious, negativistic thoughts? Do they evaporate or magically disappear? No, God constructed our brains so that these self-thoughts lie dormant or sleeping in our memories, only to wake up and re-appear if we return to self-focus. God never intends for these anxious, negativistic thoughts to overwhelm us. They are simply reminders to run back into his arms and give him our sensory focus again. Unfortunately, many of us still allow these toxic thoughts to overtake us, even though God has given us a wonderful escape route through sensory focus on him. As discussed in the next chapter, many of us fall prey to earthly addictions as our sensory escape from our ongoing pit-stops in anxious, negativistic thinking.

The sad reality is that so many people continue to allow their anxious, negativistic thinking to overtake them time and time again throughout their lives. I was sixty years old before I saw and fully embraced God's pathway for a heavenly escape. This was not because God kept his escape route secret! I simply spent a lifetime blinded by cultural and religious prescriptions for self-performance.

Obviously, God never intended me to fix this problem on my own. He also never intended for me to rely on my earthly addictions, to which I sacrificed my life for so many years. If my self-performance and earthly addictions did the trick, there would be no need for God to rescue and fix me. Only God could save me from myself. Because he knew this, he allowed his son to suffer a cruel, agonizing death on the cross at Calvary as proof that he would not hold me responsible to fix myself. In fact, Christ's death was proof that there is absolutely nothing we can do to save ourselves. God made one and only one offer, but what an incredible offer!

God not only extended his unconditional love to us by saving us through Christ, he also offered us a lifetime pass to his presence, guaranteeing that if we let him, he will take over responsibility for running our lives. He promises that if we surrender our thoughts to him, he will set us free from our old patterns of thinking and give us a new life of faith in him.

This faith is a powerful, life-changing force. *The Message* declares in Matthew 17:20 "that if you had a mere kernel of faith, a poppy seed, you could move mountains." God, in his infinite grace and wisdom, designed our brains in such a brilliant fashion that the simple choice to focus on him would activate faith strong enough to move mountains. How incredible! Shifting our sensory attention to him is a simple choice on our part that inspires God to move mountains in our lives. All God asks us to do is look his way.

Through simply dedicating our sensory attention to him, the first and biggest mountain in our lives that God moves is our anxious, negativistic thinking, and the shame that tags along close behind. God implodes this mountain when we maintain our gaze on him. In its place, he plants a beautiful garden valley full of his heavenly thoughts, where we are free to roam and play.

While the distinction may seem obvious between our huge mountain of ugly thoughts and his beautiful garden valley of divine thoughts, our many years of futility trying to climb our own mountain can make the view of the beautiful garden seem very blurry at times. The following are ten toxic thoughts from Dr. Leaf (2016) that can really cloud our vision when it comes to embracing God's uplifting thoughts:

1. How many 'could have', 'would have', 'should have' statements have you made today?

2. How many 'if only's' were part of your vocabulary today?

3. How many times have you replayed in your head a conversation or situation that pained you, or one that hasn't occurred yet?

4. How many scenarios have you created of the unpredictable future?

5. How much time is speculation taking out of your day?

6. How passive is your mind?

7. How honest are you with yourself?

8. Are you at cross-purposes with yourself-going through the motions, but not really committed to the goal, saying one thing but meaning another?

9. How distorted is your thinking? Are you forming a personal identity around for example, a disease? Do you speak about 'my arthritis', 'my multiple sclerosis', 'my heart problem'?

10. Do you ever make comments like 'nothing ever goes right for me'; everything I touch fails'; 'I always mess up'?

When I review this list and my distorted thinking interacts with these toxic thoughts, my first reaction is: "I have been guilty of all ten of these over and over again my entire life." My personal identity has been chiseled out and shaped by my sick thinking. I know I am not alone in this. Over my years of working with my clients, I have witnessed a litany of toxicity that includes thoughts like these:

> I am good for nothing.
> I am such a loser.
> I can never please her.
> I must be crazy.
> I am a complete failure.
> I am unlovable.
> Nobody cares.
> I am so stupid.
> Nobody likes me.
> I have no friends.
> Everything is my fault.
> I can't do anything right.

This list could go on and on. It's a good illustration of how we end up labeling ourselves and living in defeat when we rely on our own anxious, negativistic thinking. The great news is that God's list of uplifting thoughts is infinite and can defeat our own thinking when we simply choose to give him our sensory focus. The simple choice to give him the attention of our five senses silences our toxic thoughts and allows God's wonderful thoughts to interact with our terrible self-perception and give us a whole new identity in Christ.

The Message says in Psalm 139:17-18 "Your thoughts—how rare, how beautiful! God, I'll never comprehend them! I couldn't even begin to count them—any more than I could count the sands of the sea." God's thoughts are endless, and as we absorb how God feels about us over time, he transforms our identity into his likeness.

Not only are God's thoughts endless, they are fresh and new every day. *The Message* says in Lamentations 3:22-23 that, "God's loyal love couldn't have run out, his merciful love couldn't have dried up. They're new every morning. How great is your faithfulness!" I am so thankful that God can refresh me every morning with his thoughts when I give him my sensory focus. When I used to wake up focused on myself, it would seem that there were new negative thoughts to add to my already ample supply. On many days, the combination of my old and new negative thoughts would become all-consuming. I would dwell on myself all day long! Now, I have become fascinated with how all-consuming God's thoughts become as I live with my sensory focus on him. Psalm 111:2-3 says in *The Message* that "God's works are so great, worth a lifetime of study—endless enjoyment!" I used to wake up in the middle of the night feeling so anxious and negative. Now, when I wake up in the middle of the night, God gives me one of his delightful thoughts. "I get up in the middle of the night to thank you; your decisions are so right, so true—I can't wait until morning!" (Psalm 119:62, *The Message*).

Being excited to get up in the morning is brand new to me, because I used to be so consumed with anxious negativity that I dreaded the arrival of morning. I am so relieved that I can totally depend on God's thoughts not to be a mere reflection of my own dreaded negativity. God assures me that his thoughts are as high up in the sky as mine are down in the pits. "I don't think the way you think. The way you work isn't the way I work, God's Decree. For as the sky soars high above the earth, so the way I work surpasses the way you work, and the way I think is beyond the way you think" (Isaiah 55:8-9, *The Message).*

Wow! I am so thankful for this promise in God's Word. I became so worn out and undone from my own thinking. I reached the end of the line where I hated my own thoughts and they would not shut up. After all these years, I have finally been shown a way for my thoughts to be silenced. With my five senses fixed on God, my thoughts are quiet and I can clearly hear God's thoughts ringing in my ears. Now, God is the one who never shuts up! I love his constant attention. The following are just ten samples of God's infinite supply of thoughts for my life:

1. "Oh yes, you shaped me first inside, then out;
        you formed me in my mother's womb.
    I thank you, High God—you're breathtaking!
        Body and soul, I am marvelously made!"
            (Psalm 139:13-14, *The Message*).

2. "What's the price of two or three pet canaries? Some loose change, right? But God never overlooks a single one. And he pays even greater attention to you, down to the last detail—even numbering the hairs on your head! So don't be intimidated by all this bully talk. You're worth more than a million canaries" (Luke 12:6-7, *The Message)*.

3. "Don't be afraid, I've redeemed you.
        I've called your name. You're mine.
    When you're in over your head, I'll be there for you.
        When you're in rough waters, you will not go down.
    When you're between a rock and a hard place,
        it won't be a dead end—
    Because I am God, your personal God,
        The Holy of Israel, your Savior.
    I paid a huge price for you:
        all of Egypt, with rich Cush and Seba thrown in.
    That's how much you mean to me!

That's how much I love you!
I'd sell off the whole world to get you back,
   trade the creation just for you"
      (Isaiah 43:2-4, *The Message).*

4. "I've picked you. I haven't dropped you.
   Don't panic. I'm with you.
      There's no need for fear for I'm your God.
   I'll give you strength. I'll help you.
      I'll hold you steady, keep a firm grip on you"
         (Isaiah 41:9-10, *The Message*).

5. "But for you who welcome him, in whom he dwells—
even though you experience all the limitations of sin—you
yourself experience life on God's terms. It stands to reason,
doesn't it, that if the alive-and-present God who raised
Jesus from the dead moves into your life, he'll do the same
thing in you that he did in Jesus, bringing you alive to
himself? When God lives and breathes in you (and he does
as surely as he did in Jesus) you are delivered from that
dead life. With his Spirit living in you, your body will be as
alive as Christ's!" (Romans 8:10-11, *The Message*).

6. "Hey there! All you who are thirsty,
      come to the water!
   Are you penniless?
      Come anyway—buy and eat!
   Come, buy your drinks, buy wine and milk.
      Buy without money—everything's free!
   Pay attention, come close now,
      listen carefully to my life-giving,
      life-nourishing words.
   I'm making a lasting covenant with you,
      the same that I made with David:

sure, solid, enduring love"
(Isaiah 55:1, 3, *The Message*).

7. "God's Spirit spoke through me, his words took shape on my tongue. The God of Israel's Rock-Mountain said, 'Whoever governs fairly and well, who rules in the Fear-of-God, is like first light at daybreak without a cloud in the sky, like green grass carpeting earth, glistening under fresh rain.' And this is how my regime has been, for God guaranteed its covenant with me, spelled it out plainly and kept every promised word—my entire salvation, my every desire" (2 Samuel 23:2-5, *The Message*).

8. "Trust God from the bottom of your heart; don't try to figure out everything on your own. Listen for God's voice in everything you do, everywhere you go; he's the one who will keep you on track. Don't assume that you know it all. Run to God! Run from evil! Your body will glow with health, your very bones will vibrate with life" (Proverbs 3:5-8, *The Message*).

9. "With the arrival of Jesus, the Messiah, that fateful dilemma is resolved. Those who enter into Christ's-being-here-for-us no longer have to live under a continuous, low-lying black cloud. A new power is in operation. The Spirit of life in Christ, like a strong wind, has magnificently cleared the air, freeing you from a fated lifetime of brutal tyranny at the hands of sin and death" (Romans 8:1-2, *The Message*).

10. "Do you see what you've got? An unshakable kingdom! And do you see how thankful we must be? Not only thankful, but brimming with worship, deeply reverent before God. For God is not an indifferent bystander. He's

actively cleaning house, torching all that needs to burn, he won't quit until it's cleansed. God himself is fire!" (Hebrews 12:28-29, *The Message*).

This final scripture sums up everything so well when comparing God's thoughts about me to my own anxious, negativistic thoughts about myself. I can recall the thousands of times I quit on myself throughout my life. Even though I knew I was failing, I would repeatedly return to trying on my own again, going back to my performance-driven efforts to run my own life. These self-driven attempts repeatedly ended with the same disastrous results.

But guess what? I never have to try on my own again! I can permanently retire from the job of running my own life, because God keeps his promise never to quit on me. I have embraced this truth with my whole heart, so that when the thought of relying on myself even crosses my mind, I simply use it as a reminder to put my sensory focus on God instead.

Consider the joy expressed in Psalm 118:1-4: "Thank God because he's good, because his love never quits. Tell the world, Israel, 'His love never quits.' And you who fear God, join in, 'his love never quits'" (*The Message*). If this is true, why do so many of us struggle along in the rut of self-reliance, ignoring God's offer to run our lives for us? One reason is that we often get fooled by our cultural heritage of fierce independence. Even many of our churches have adopted this cultural heritage down through the ages, spouting doctrine that boils down to "God helps those who help themselves." We are taught over and over again to straighten out our own thoughts and our own lives. This teaching is at the core of most educational, occupational, spiritual and even therapeutic training endeavors.

However, this teaching stands in outright opposition to what the Bible teaches, and ignores how God created our brain. How many times has someone in authority reprimanded us by saying, "God gave you a brain, now use it"? Unfortunately, the authorities who toss around that cliché have no idea themselves how God designed the brain!

We need solid teaching on how God designed the brain. We need to go back to the Bible to see that independent thinking is not at the core of learning how to live our lives. Many of us understand at some level that it would be a great idea to dig deep into how God made the brain and to dig deep into God's word, but we never get around to it. Often we are too busy running our own lives to stop and be totally open to what God teaches. My openness did not begin until I was desperate to quit on myself (again) at the ripe young age of about sixty years old.

I often tell my clients in the beginning that sensory focus on God and letting him run their lives is like eating food with the "wrong" hand. It feels so unfamiliar at first. Scripture tells us something very similar in *The Message* in Hebrews 12:6-12 where it says: "God is educating you; that's why you must never drop out. He's treating you as dear children. This trouble you're in isn't punishment. It is training, the normal experience of children. Only irresponsible parents leave children to fend for themselves. Would you prefer an irresponsible God? We respect our own parents for training and not spoiling us, so why not embrace God's training so we can truly live? While we were children, our parents did what seemed best for them. But God is doing what is best for us, training us to live God's holy best. At the time, discipline isn't much fun. It always feels like it's going against the grain. Later, of course, it pays off handsomely, for it's the well-trained who find themselves mature in their relationship with God."

God is so committed to doing what is best for us that he literally wants to think for us. This radical offer on his part goes against every grain of our being, because we have been so conditioned to do our own thinking. Many of us have had reliance on self-thinking pounded into our brains from the day we were born. Even as children, many of us were scolded for mistakes with the words "think before you act!" We have been brainwashed into believing that *more thinking* is what causes us to succeed or fail in life. We are also often reminded that our five senses are not reliable, or even evil, and that we must employ corrective thinking to straighten out our lives. Endless books have been written about correcting thought patterns, and many of us have attended seminars in an attempt to better understand and improve our thinking. Often, this teaching emphasizes not relying on what experts have erroneously labeled "fickle feelings." I sincerely hope that this book makes a significant impact in our present-day culture and churches and changes this modern-day madness of teaching all of us to disregard our sensory brains. To continue this madness would result in even more sensory deprivation and separation from God's love.

Here is a 21st-century, radical revelation: God did not design our brains to think for themselves. He clearly doesn't *want* us to think for ourselves. He describes our negative thoughts as naturally evil and degenerate. This is one way we know that we are the author of those thoughts and not God. I have spent so much time with my own nasty thoughts that now they jump out at me with a vengeance, standing in stark contrast to the thoughts God gives me. I hate my own thoughts now, especially since God's thoughts are always so encouraging, caring, compassionate, loving, and uplifting.

It took me several months to fully embrace God's thoughts in me after I chose to immerse myself in his thoughts throughout every day. What God showed me in those few months and every day since then, is that I used to credit myself for all those amazing thoughts that he authored. Until I devoted my sensory focus to him and he showed me that he is the author of everything good in my life, I was giving myself total credit. In my own self-absorption and sensory focus on me, I kept believing the lie that I could save myself—even though I set a record for losing every battle in my relentless attempts to win the war against myself.

Only God is capable of winning the war over who runs our lives because he constructed our brains with the capacity to give him the complete attention of our five senses, which he uses to draw our mental attention totally away from our own thoughts. That empties the thinking side of our brain to fill up with his thoughts, while the sensory side of our brain is engrossed in him. Any doubters of this new mystery revealed and supported by recent brain discoveries can have their doubts silenced by engaging in a sensory activity and witness how their own thoughts quickly fade away.

Never forget that God was the original brain scientist who designed this miracle in life. In his architecture of the brain, God precisely created us so that he only requires our sensory focus on him to activate his thinking on the logical side of our brain. He intentionally designed our brains in this intricately constructed way so he could run our lives for us. In fact, total sensory focus on him silences our own thought waves, so they do not make noise and interfere with our reception of his thoughts.

In spite of God's incomparable offer to think for us and run our lives, people everywhere still insist on working harder than ever in their futile attempts to figure out and fix their own problems. Their continual efforts only cause more problems—long mountainous ranges of anxious negativity. This negative thinking, which stems from our chronic overuse of the thinking side of the brain, presents itself in many forms. Toxic thinking can present itself as panic or chronic worry and mental obsession. It can also cause depression from the mind wearing itself out, or rage when anxious thinking flips to anger.

Regardless of how self-thinking is exhibited, the long-term outcome is a brain that is stuck on the same radio station of continual head noise and mental static. This chronic state of feeling stuck in our thoughts causes mental contortions and takes people through such awful torment that they feel like they are losing their minds or going crazy. They experience an explosion of irrational thoughts, all firing at once. They feel like they can never relax or have any peace of mind. At this point, they feel totally deflated, broken, unfixable and hopeless. They experience so much mental pressure that they reach the end of their rope and even want to quit on life. Their thoughts reach such an unbearable high pitch that it seems like the only possible solution is to die.

In addition to mental torment, many people riddled with anxious, negativistic thinking experience various physical symptoms. Negativity has been long recognized as a major contributor to illnesses and diseases, some of which are life-threatening. More commonly, anxious, negativistic thinking causes lots of physical discomfort and various bodily tensions and chronic pain. Clients who experience lots of these thoughts often report chest pressure and tightness. A client of mine who struggled with anxiety once told me she felt like there was a truck sitting on her chest. Her previous therapist had told her to take a deep breath when she experienced this chest pain. When I heard this, my immediate reaction was to think that it could be catastrophic to suggest someone try to take a deep breath with a truck already crushing their lungs. Instead of telling her to try calming herself down, I took my client for a brief walk around the small lake next to my office. The rhythmic pace of the walk and seeing the ducks and turtles captured her sensory attention. The intense pressure on her chest was completely gone after about a hundred yards.

When someone reaches these desperate states of anxious, negativistic thinking, this can be a life-changing opportunity to reach out to God. Simply by making the choice to turn our total sensory focus to God, we can start down the path of total trust, depending on him every moment of each day for the rest of our lives.

God designed our brains with a wonderful built-in capacity to relax from intense mental pressure through a brain bridge spanning from the logical side to the sensory side of our brain. However, barely anyone has been educated about God's genius in how he designed the brain in this fashion. Even worse, many people have been shamed for not having the courage to abandon themselves to God and trust in him. Fortunately, crossing the brain bridge and trusting in God through sensory focus has nothing to do with courage. Unfortunately, almost no one in our churches has ever been taught anything about the brain, let alone how to cross the brain bridges to relieve mental torment through putting our sensory focus on God.

Because of their lack of education about the brain, church leaders literally don't know what to do when people reach out to the church to be shown how to get relief from their mental torment. The only thing church leaders know what to say to people stuck in anxious negativity is to try even harder to fix their thinking. They convince people to put even more mental effort into their religious practices, such as reading the Bible or prayer, in order to relieve their anxiety.

Let's think about this more carefully. When a person who suffers with anxiety-induced chest pain prays for God to relieve their anxiety and then checks to see if their chest pain has gone away, they are usually keenly aware that their chest still hurts. Their focus is on their chest pain and on their anxious thought patterns, not on God. At this point, a church leader might encourage them to pray harder, or pray with more faith. When this does not work, this person in physical pain can easily feel abandoned or even punished by God for not being good enough. Of course, as to be expected, these feelings of failure and rejection cause even more anxious, negativistic thinking and also its close companions: guilt and shame. However, if someone in the church simply had the knowledge to teach the discouraged, defeated person how to put their sensory focus on God, the chest pain would go away and the anxiety, guilt, and shame would be held in check.

One client with chest pain told me that his favorite time with God was playing hymns on the trumpet. I suggested that playing these hymns was an ideal sensory prayer that would completely take his focus off his chest, thereby removing his chest pain. Playing his trumpet involved four of his five senses, sight, sound, taste and touch. This intense focus on the sensory side of the brain totally replaced his focus on any thoughts that made his chest hurt. My client experienced fast relief from any chest pressure caused by these thoughts. The anxious, negativistic thoughts were completely released as his full sensory attention was drawn to playing the trumpet.

God has endless sensory solutions for relieving anxious, negativistic thinking—solutions that very few people use, because they have never been taught about them. God's design for our brains to be able to quickly cross a bridge from anxious, negativistic thinking to sensory-focus relief is fascinating. This discovery provides so much hope for the treatment of toxic thoughts in our performance-driven society.

It is so exciting to read the Bible along with reading about the brain. The Bible and the brain as sources for new hope for the downtrodden are incredibly similar in their teachings. Hopefully, many people will read this book and learn that only God can progressively heal their troubled lives through sensory focus on him. I am labeling this sensory pursuit of God "Heavenly Addiction." Until we learn how heavenly addiction works, we will continue to be vulnerable to earthly addictions in our desperate human efforts for relief from our anxiety, negativistic thinking.

"I'll never forget the trouble, the utter lostness, the taste of ashes, the poison I've swallowed. I remember it all—oh, how I remember the feeling of hitting bottom" (Lamentations 3:19-20, *The Message*).

Chapter Three

Earthly Addictions

*"Some of you wandered for years in the desert,
looking but not finding a good place to live . . . staggering
and stumbling, on the brink of exhaustion. Then, in your
desperate condition, you called out to GOD . . . He put
your feet on a wonderful road that took you straight to a
good place to live. So thank GOD for his marvelous love. . .
He poured great draughts of water down parched throats;
the starved and the hungry got plenty to eat."*

- Psalm 107:4-9, *The Message*

Between the formative stages of anxious,
negativistic thinking and the ultimate stage of total burnout,
human beings often suffer through many years of desperate
attempts to escape their mental prisons through earthly
addictions. Although addictions have traditionally been
viewed as either moral or mental weaknesses, in clinical
language, addictions are more accurately defined as
unhealthy coping mechanisms for miserable thinking.
When our thinking mind becomes overloaded with racing
thoughts and anxious negativity, many people are drawn to
the temporary sensory relief and escape that earthly
addictions provide.

Almost anything taken to an extreme can become an
addiction. Some common examples of addictions that are
sensory escapes from anxious thinking are gaming

addictions, binge eating and other food or eating disorders, shopping sprees, pornography and other sexual addictions, social media and other internet addictions, casino, sports and online wagering or gambling, nicotine, caffeine, and alcohol, to say nothing of the vast varieties of drug addictions.

While playing a video game, scrolling through Facebook, going shopping, eating food or enjoying a glass of wine are not destructive in moderation, far too many people get hooked on certain outlets for temporary sensory escapes, which can easily become ways to avoid the normal routines of life, work, school, family, and leisure time. Over time, addicts' whole lives start to revolve around their addictions, and more and more of their time is spent looking for their next fix.

One of the symptoms of addiction involves the addict using over and over again, trying to achieve a high. This recurrent use results in tolerance, a condition in which the body and brain adjust to increasing levels of a drug or activity, until not even excessive use can create the desired effect. Tolerance leads to changes in physical brain structure, until our brains need to feed the addicition not just to achieve a high, but to feel normal and prevent the devastating symptoms of withdrawal.

The American Psychiatric Association includes the increased tolerance factor in their criteria for characterizing internet gaming disorders (Petry, Nancy. et. al., 2014). The nine criteria include factors that could be applied to almost every addictive disorder:

1. Pre-occupation. Do you spend a lot of time thinking about games even when you are not playing, or planning when you can play next?

2. Withdrawal. Do you feel restless, irritable, moody, anxious or sad when attempting to cut down or stop gaming, or when you are unable to play?

3. Tolerance. Do you feel the need to play for increasing amounts of time, play more exciting games, or use more powerful equipment to get the same amount of excitement you used to get?

4. Reduce/stop. Do you feel that you should play less, but are unable to cut back on the amount of time you spend playing games?

5. Give up other activities. Do you lose interest in or reduce participation in other recreational activities (hobbies, meetings with friends) due to gaming?

6. Continue despite problems. Do you continue to play games even though you are aware of negative consequences, such as not getting enough sleep, being late to school/work, spending too much money, having arguments with others. Or neglecting important duties?

7. Deceive/cover up. Do you lie to family, friends or others about how much you game, or try to keep your family or friends from knowing how much you game?

8. Escape adverse moods. Do you game to escape from or

forget about personal problems, or to relieve uncomfortable feelings such as guilt, anxiety, helplessness or depression?

9. Risk/lose relationships/opportunities. Do you risk or lose significant relationships, or job, educational or career opportunities because of gaming?

These questions speak volumes about how an addiction can take over your life and have a detrimental impact in virtually every possible way. This is true not only with the classic alcohol and drug addictions, but also with more non-traditional behavioral addictions like gaming addiction.

Like many of the more well-known earthly addictions, gaming addiction has resulted in the formation of a self-help group, called Online Gamers Anonymous (OGA). Like most self-help groups, OGA is a 12-step program that focuses on helping its members and their families through accountability and support for quitting online gaming. Although the word "self-help" is a standard label for these anonymous recovery groups, in reality the participants learn to reach out to other members and no longer rely on themselves and their own thinking to get better. Participants also feel a sense of acceptance and belonging because other members have gone through very similar addictive experiences. They feel less shame and guilt in these anonymous settings than they do in the everyday world of high performance expectations and strong judgement.

Because so much of our mainstream world has always been extremely performance-driven, many people outside of these anonymous groups begin to criticize and shame the person who is suffering from earthly addictions. Everyone seems to notice how the person is spending more and more time running away from life's typical responsibilities. These same people fail to see behind the scenes of the person's life to what may be causing them to escape through various addictions. Because of the criticism and shame assigned to people whose earthly addictive escapes get out of hand, addicts often withdraw to keep their addictive outlets a secret. Trying to hide an addictive habit can become a full time job, causing even more underlying anxiety and negative thinking. As a result, the buildup of shame over and escape through addictions becomes a vicious cycle of daily living. This cycle keeps intensifying until we are staggering and stumbling and on the brink of exhaustion. At this point, it is quite common for a hurting person to turn to church leaders or counselors as their way of calling out to God.

God definitely wants us to turn to him and invite him to run our lives and rid us of shame, anxiety, and earthly addictions. Unfortunately, when we turn to a church leader or even a typical Christian counselor, we are often led further down the path of trying to think our way out of problems, rather than being directed toward the sensory path with God as the center of our attention. Far too often, when we finally come to the end of our rope and we are ready and willing to let God take over our lives, the people we turn to for help are only able to show us how to turn back to our own human efforts and try harder than ever to pull ourselves back from the brink of disaster. That was my primary way as a Christian counselor of trying to help people up until about four years ago, when God showed me a new way of life and a new therapy that would actually teach others how to focus on God to run their lives instead of remaining stuck in self-focus.

Just like our futile efforts to figure out and fix our personal problems can build mountains of anxious, negativistic thinking, the many addictions that we turn to in our attempts to relieve anxiety can become huge mountains themselves. What all earthly addictions have in common is their own built-in thinking addiction. Addicted people become fixated on their thoughts about their "drug of choice." Mountainous addictions are just as problematic as anxiety itself and can generate even more anxious, negativistic thinking. Earthly addictions have serious and lasting negative consequences in the addict's life and the lives of their family and friends. Mountains of shame and guilt begin to pile up as well as our lives fall apart. The addict becomes so hyper-focused on getting their next high that they become helpless to get help at a human level. There are too many mental mountains, and they are too high and steep to climb. Fortunately, God never intended for there to be a human cure for earthly addictions, or the shame and guilt that go along for the ride. His one and only cure is sensory hyper-focus on him: becoming a heavenly addict.

God spells out this cure in *The Message*, Ephesians 5:18-20 where these words are written: "Don't drink too much wine. That cheapens your life. Drink the Spirit of God, huge draughts of him. Sing hymns instead of drinking songs! Sing songs from your heart to Christ. Sing praises over everything, any excuse for a song to God the Father in the name of our Master, Jesus Christ." These verses clearly instruct us to drink God (heavenly addiction) instead of wine (earthly addiction). These verses even show us how to drink God by singing praises over everything. This is how we devote our sensory focus to God.

When we devote our sensory focus to God, he builds a longing in us for his love that leaves our desires for earthly addictions in the dust. He guarantees this longing for him even during hard times. He promises that nothing and no one can override our longing for him when we keep our sensory focus on his love. This means that dwelling in his love through focus on him with our five senses will safeguard us from going back to anxiety and earthly addictions even during the most difficult of seasons in our lives. Even when we have moments of focus relapse and take our eyes off him, the incredible love we have experienced in him will pull us back into his arms like a magnetic force. We will not be able to stand to be separated from his love anymore. As a heavenly addict, we will progress to the point where it becomes unbearable to leave God's side.

From my own personal experience with God over the past several years, I have become so relieved that I can simply choose to keep my sensory focus on him and depend on him to tell me and show me what to say and what action to take in every area of my life. What a relief it is not to have to figure out life on my own anymore! I have countless examples of how God clearly shows me what decision to make and what action to take at exactly the right time. He not only shows me what to do and when, He shows me how. Often I don't understand why he directs me the way he does, but I'm okay with that. The why questions always move me back over to my logical brain and I naturally begin to try to figure things out on my own again. The why questions take me back to my brain's own thinking center and distract me from my sensory focus on him. From a sensory standpoint, it has become unbearable to leave his side. I don't trust myself and I don't trust my own thinking. I long to live all the time now in his reality, not my own reality anymore.

The Message says in Matthew 6:30-34: "If God gives such attention to the appearance of wild flowers—most of which are never seen—don't you think he'll attend to you, take pride in you, do his best for you? What I'm trying to do here is get you to relax, to not be so preoccupied with getting, so you can respond to God's giving. People who don't know God and the way he works fuss over these things, but you know God and how he works. Steep your life in God-reality, God-initiative, God provisions. Don't worry about missing out. You'll find all your everyday human concerns will be met. Give your entire attention to what God is doing right now, and don't get worked up about what may or may not happen tomorrow. God will help you deal with whatever hard things come up when the time comes."

Giving our entire attention to what God is doing right now is a great definition of what it means to give God the full focus of all five of our senses in the moment. When *The Message* instructs us to steep our life in God-reality, it is referring to the Hebrew definition of *steep* as a verb, which is "to immerse, engulf, plunge, engross, absorb, soak up, focus." These words are all powerfully descriptive of what it means to give God the full attention of our five senses in the moment. Only when we immerse ourselves in

God's reality with our five senses can we feel completely safe and free from ourselves and our own efforts.

When we absorb ourselves in God in this sensory way, he continually shows us that his love is unconditional, unimaginable and unbreakable. Today or tomorrow, he will never abandon us, not ever. Romans 8:35 and 37-39 says, "Do you think anyone is going to be able to drive a wedge between us and Christ's love for us? There is no way! Not trouble, not hard times, not hatred, not hunger, not homelessness, not bullying threats, not backstabbing . . . None of this fazes us because Jesus loves us. I'm absolutely convinced that nothing—nothing living or dead, angelic or demonic, today or tomorrow, high or low, thinkable or unthinkable—absolutely nothing can get between us and God's love because of the way that Jesus our Master has embraced us" (*The Message*).

David, in the Psalms, according to *The Message* in chapter 131, verses 1-2, embraced the Master's love when he wrote: "God, I'm not trying to rule the roost . . . I haven't meddled where I have no business . . . I've cultivated a quiet heart, [like] a baby content in its mother's arms, my soul is a baby content." God inspired David to describe man's ideal relationship with God as identical to a baby lodged safely in his mother's arms. Babies' brains operate totally in the sensory, they are too young to be able to think for themselves. They are totally dependent on their mothers to care for them and make all decisions on their behalf. God wants us to become like little babies when we choose to put our faith in him and call him our Heavenly Father. God desires us to cling to him with all our senses so he can do all our thinking and decision-making for us.

Despite these amazing scriptures that were written centuries ago, most people still have not devoted their senses to God so they can become heavenly addicts, steeped in God's reality. They are still clinging on to their self-knowledge on the thinking side of their brain and also clinging onto their shame on the sensory side of their brain. This leaves them wide open to earthly addictions that are on display everywhere around the world in endless shapes and sizes, including porn and beer at convenience stores to pills of all colors at local pharmacies. Almost anything can qualify as an addiction. Food, money, clothes, shoes, and drugs, to name only a few, are sensory items people fall in love with and use as an escape from the stress of life. In and of themselves, some of these items are not even harmful; however, taken to the extreme they can captivate the time and attention in any of us to the degree of extreme sensory hyper-focus. When we are not steeped in a heavenly addiction with God, we are easy targets and totally vulnerable to become trapped in earthly addictions.

Trying to run our own lives and not devoting our entire attention to God guarantees that earthly addictions will be the outcome of our efforts. *The Message* says in Galatians 5:19-21 that "It is obvious what kind of life develops out of trying to get your own way all the time: repetitive, loveless, cheap sex; a stinking accumulation of mental and emotional garbage; frenzied and joyless grabs for happiness; trinket gods, magic-show religion; paranoid loneliness; cutthroat competition; all-consuming-yet-never-satisfied wants; a brutal temper; an impotence to love or be loved; divided homes and divided lives; small-minded and lopsided pursuits; the vicious habit of depersonalizing everyone into a rival; uncontrolled and uncontrollable addictions . . . "

What all earthly addictions have in common is a high degree of sensory appeal or attractiveness through one or more of our five senses. Since the sensory side of the brain gets bombarded with shame, many people are "sitting ducks," just waiting for addictions to invade the vast wasteland of their sensory brains. Their brains are starving for intense sensory stimulation and addictions are lying in wait to provide a quick fix through immediate gratification. In no time at all our sensory brains are feasting on these appetizing addictions. They make us feel so good in the moment that our sensory shame and anxious thoughts fade far into the background. Our distorted human reasoning becomes certain that a great human cure has been found for our sensory deprivation.

That is, until, time passes and the highs become lows. The alcohol becomes a depressant. The sugar high wears off. The casino takes all our money. Our spouse catches us watching porn. We gain fifty pounds, or spend all our money on clothes or that new boat we never use. The list of negative consequences could go on and on, far exceeding any quickly fading high we received at the beginning of our addiction. Even worse, all of these negative consequences cause even greater shame and anxiety in our daily lives. The whole time, our thinking brain is constructing a mental prison that we become stuck in with no way of escape except attempting to keep digging underground to find another earthly addiction that will keep us distracted from our own self-loathing.

People can go through many different addictions, each time falling for a new drug that feels like a good lover, but they can never get enough. They are an anxious mess just looking for more and more of something that can never permanently satisfy them. They experience lust, which can drive them to extreme measures to satisfy their cravings. These cravings cause them all kinds of problems in multiple dimensions of their everyday lives. Even Christians go to these extreme measures to satisfy their lust, in spite of Paul's warning in Galatians 5:21 that "this is not the first time I have warned you, you know. If you use your freedom this way, you will not inherit God's kingdom" (*The Message*).

The Bible makes it crystal clear that the problem is our choice to focus on doing things our way versus making the choice to put our sensory focus on God so we can live his way. Paul certainly was clear about the dramatic difference between running our own lives and God running our lives. Paul was himself the recipient of a radical conversion on the road to Damascus, turned from killing followers of Christ to leading people to Christ. Listen to how he continues in Galatians 5:22-23: "But what happens when we live God's way? He brings gifts into our lives, much the same way that fruit appears in an orchard—things like affection for others, exuberance about life, serenity. We develop a willingness to stick with things. A sense of compassion in the heart, and a conviction that a basic holiness permeates things and people. We find ourselves involved in loyal commitments, not needing to force our way in life . . ."

God designed our brain to desire more and more of him when we place our sensory focus on him. As we desire more and more of his love, he totally meets our needs to feel loved and cared for. His love is always enough—it is a permanent fix! As long as we choose to keep our sensory focus on him, we don't even want to go back to fixing things ourselves. As Paul says in *The Message*, Galatians 6:14-16, we want "to boast about nothing but the Cross of our Master, Jesus Christ. Because of that cross, I have been crucified in relation to the world, set free from the stifling atmosphere of pleasing others and fitting into the little patterns that they dictate. Can't you see the central issue in all this? It is not what you and I do—submit to circumcision, reject circumcision. It is what God is doing, and he is creating something totally new, a free life!"

When we choose to devote our sensory focus to God, he creates in us a whole new life of freedom. However, God still gives us the choice to focus on either our way or his way; and, we will not inherit his kingdom and experience this new free life in him when we choose our way. Our senses will be doomed to focus on earthly addictions and our brain will be doomed to experience more and more lust, not love. Our brain thrives on habits and when it is repeatedly trained to indulge in earthly addictions, it is not willing to refrain simply because we or anyone else scolds us for our earthly obsessions. Our brain will always find a way to escape to the earthly addiction it has been trained to enjoy and rely on for comfort, a way of relieving stress, boredom, hurt, and pain.

At first, with any earthly addiction, our brain is tricked into feeling that the addiction is like the ultimate relationship. In the moment of getting high the user can feel accepted, loved and cared for by the drug. But this is merely the outcome of lust. No amount is ever enough. No earthly addiction can satisfy a person's basic human needs to feel loved and cared for. These are emotional needs as basic as our physical needs for food, water and shelter. The needs of our five senses can never be fulfilled by any type of earthly addiction. Only God can fulfill the basic physical and emotional needs of our five senses. Even then, he can only fulfill them when we continually choose to give him the focus of our five senses.

For as long as anyone stays on the road of tunneling underground into the world of addictions, every road leads to the same dead end: the mental prison of anxious, negativistic thinking and shame. Many clients wait to come see me until they reach this dead end. They get to the point where they can barely sleep, or can barely taste their food anymore, or are afraid to leave their house, or can't stop raging or crying—their suffering is more than they can bear. They remind me of hoarders, who are so run over by their clutter, they give up. Hoarders lose a sense of direction about where and how to start their cleanup, because their clutter builds all the way up to the ceiling and even blocks doorways.

Like hoarders, many addicts deteriorate to the point where they experience great anxiety and worry. They are embarrassed by the stigma of their addiction, refusing to allow others to see the mess their lives have become. They begin to feel very awkward in social situations and their addictive behavior leads to isolation from family, friends, and society. They are, in effect, mental hoarders. Their minds are so cluttered that they feel trapped in the junk-filled rooms of their minds. All they know how to do is cling to their anxious, negativistic thinking.

Addicts come to falsely believe that their addictions are an extension of themselves. Eventually even their shame no longer stems from their actions—simply their daily existence is enough to induce shame. They so badly want to let go of their addictions and shame, yet are totally unaware of how to relax without getting high or taking a drug to calm down. One young man was in such bad mental shape that he begged me to stop the explosions in his head. He was ecstatic when I was able to stop the panic fireworks for four minutes simply with the "Magic Piano" app on my iPad.

Some clinicians would claim that these anxiety prisoners of war are beyond therapeutic help and need medication. I do agree that medication can be helpful, but mostly I believe that the end of the road is finally the miracle moment when a person totally gives up trying to fix themselves and becomes willing to put their hope in God. They finally accept there is no anxiety cure, no thought cure, no addiction cure, no shame cure—no human cure whatsoever. They realize that God is all they have left, and then they are ready to believe that sensory focus on God is the only cure possible. Their only hope is to become a heavenly addict. Otherwise, they are left paralyzed as a vast sea of shame continues to rise, and they experience the horrible feeling that they are about to go under and drown in their own misery.

"Then you called out to God in your desperate condition; he got you out in the nick of time. He spoke the word that healed you, that pulled you back from the brink of death. So thank God for his marvelous love" (Psalm 107:19-21, *The Message*).

Hopefully, many people will read this book and learn that only God can progressively heal their troubled lives through sensory focus on him. I am labeling this sensory pursuit of God "Heavenly Addiction." Until we learn how heavenly addiction works, we will continue to be vulnerable to earthly addictions in their desperate human efforts for sensory escape and to feel better.

"I'll never forget the trouble, the utter lostness, the taste of ashes, the poison I've swallowed. I remember it all—oh, how I remember the feeling of hitting bottom" (Lamentations 3:19-20, *The Message*).

Chapter Four

It's All About the Shame

"When the Woman saw that the tree looked like good eating and realized what she would get out of it—she'd know everything!—she took and ate the fruit and gave some to her husband and he ate. Immediately the two of them did 'see what's really going on'—saw themselves naked! They sewed fig leaves together as makeshift clothes for themselves. When they heard the sound of God strolling in the garden in the evening breeze, the Man and his Wife hid in the trees of the garden, hid from God."

- Genesis 3:6-8, *The Message*

The initial three chapters of this book cover the deadly processes that produce shame-based living. Life has been all about the shame since the beginning of time in the Garden of Eden. Although God's original plan of creation did not include shame, man altered God's perfect design through the first sin. Shame was mankind's human response to sin. Sin and shame have gone hand in hand ever since. One does not happen without the other. The initial occurrence of sin began a never-ending cycle of sin and shame, where sin causes shame and shame drives us to more sin. This cycle was blatantly visible throughout the entire Old Testament. In the New Testament, Christ's death on the cross gave mankind a new escape route from this cycle. Through his death on the cross, Christ gave us absolution from the curse of sin and its companion, shame.

Despite God's incredible rescue plan for mankind from sin and shame, it seems that our culture and church never totally embraced this lifetime "get out of jail free" card. On the contrary, our culture and church accepted God's offer to set us free from sin and shame through Christ's death on the cross in theory only. Very few people have ever cashed in this free gift card. In fact, predominant religious practice continues to teach that shame is a necessary feeling to motivate people to not sin again. This belief is a fabrication of man, because shame doesn't keep us *from* sin, it keeps us *in* sin. Only God can free us from sin. Shame doesn't free us from anything, it only keeps us trapped in our failures.

Why would our culture and church continue to completely miss the boat on the clear teaching about shame in the Bible? One explanation is that frequently the church teachers lead in shame. They are shame-driven, sometimes even more so than the people they teach. Shame is the product of human performance efforts and leaders are frequently very high achievers. These leaders are subconsciously performance-driven and their teaching automatically follows how they live their own lives rather than what God's Word clearly says. Old leaders teach new leaders and the tradition of shame-based instruction carries on from one generation to the next at a subconscious level that goes totally unnoticed. This practice of shame hiding in the subconscious continues despite the universal body language of shame, which includes blushing, mental confusion, poor eye contact, a hunched or slumped posture, and a hanging head.

Gershen Kaufman summed up many of the consequences of shame in one paragraph of his book entitled *The Psychology of Shame*. He wrote that "shame is important because no other affect is more disturbing to the self, none more central for the sense of identity. In the context of normal development, shame is the source of low self-esteem, diminished self-image, poor self-concept, and deficient body-image. Shame itself produces self-doubt and disrupts both security and confidence. It can become an impediment to the experience of belonging and to shared intimacy. . . It is the experiential ground from which conscience and identity evolve. In pathological development, shame is central to the emergence of alienation, loneliness, inferiority and perfectionism. It plays a central role in many psychological disorders as well, including depression, paranoia, addiction, and borderline conditions. Sexual disorders and many eating disorders are largely disorders of shame. Both physical and sexual abuse also significantly involve shame" (Kaufmann, 1996, xvi).

As Kaufman wrote, among many psychological disorders, shame plays a central role in addictions. Darlene Lancer, a marriage and family therapist, also portrays shame as being at the core of addiction. In an article arguing that shame is the core of addiction and codependency, Lancer writes that "shame is so painful to the psyche that most people will do anything to avoid it, even though it's a natural emotion that everyone has. It's a physiologic response of the autonomic nervous system. You might blush, have a rapid heartbeat, break into a sweat, freeze, hang your head, slump your shoulders, avoid eye contact, withdraw, even get dizzy or nauseous" (Lancer, 2012).

In the same article, Lancer went on to explain why shame is so painful. She wrote that "shame is an intense global feeling of inadequacy, inferiority, or self-loathing. You want to hide or disappear. In front of others, you feel exposed or humiliated, as if they can see your flaws. The worst part of it is a profound sense of separation—from yourself and from others. It's disintegrating, meaning that you lose touch with all the other parts of yourself, and you also feel disconnected from everyone else. Shame induces unconscious beliefs, such as:

> I'm a failure.
> I'm not important.
> I'm unlovable.
> I don't deserve to be happy.
> I'm a bad person.
> I'm a phony.
> I'm defective."

Unconscious beliefs, such as the ones listed by Darlene Lancer, lead earthly addicts to be ashamed of who they are. Strong feelings of unworthiness and unhappiness can be so emotionally painful that addicted people feel stuck in a cycle of shame, addictive escapes, followed by more shame. There seems like no way to break free from this pain. When the pain becomes too unbearable to absorb inwardly, some people go to any length to cause pain to others through boasting, envy, ridicule or even becoming a bully. Of course, these nasty behaviors only bring on more self-loathing over the long haul. Everyone ends up feeling miserable and unhappy with no human escape from this sad predicament.

As newborn children are brought into this pitiful culture of shame, parents (governed by shame) experience great difficulty in forming close emotional attachment to their infants, which cultivates a new generation of shame-based living. Dr. Jeanne Segal and Dr. Jaelline Jaffe recently authored an article on attachment, bonding and relationships. The article features the work pioneered by English psychiatrist John Bowlby and American psychologist Mary Ainsworth on attachment bond theory. Segal and Jaffe write that attachment theory "has gained strength through worldwide scientific studies and the use of brain imaging technology that helps us understand what it takes to help build and nurture productive and meaningful relationships" (Segal and Jaffe, 2016).

Segal and Jaffe describe an attachment bond as "the term for your first interactive love relationship—the one you had with your primary caregiver as an infant, usually your mother. This mother-child attachment bond shapes an infant's brain, profoundly influencing your self-esteem, your expectations of others and your ability to attract and maintain successful adult relationships" (Segal and Jaffe, 2016). This attachment theory is fascinating, since all the interactive experiences during infancy depend on nonverbal communication, yet they determine how people will relate to others throughout their life. This theory is also alarming, considering the vast numbers of people who reside in shame-filled homes, giving birth to the next generation of shame-filled babies. Because the infant brain is so strongly influenced by the attachment bond, a primary caregiver who is very anxious, hyper-vigilant, distrusting, and/or self-loathing can prevent the newborn from developing a nervous system that becomes "securely attached." This insecure attachment can inhibit the child from being "self-confident, trusting, hopeful, and comfortable in the face of conflict" (Segal and Jaffe, 2016).

Despite these devastating consequences of shame leaking down through generations of people, many church leaders still insist on putting a shame spin on their attempts to teach godly behavior. This teaching includes Christ's death on the cross. I was taught by the church from an early age that Christ died on the cross for my sins, so I should feel terrible because I didn't let his death keep me from practicing more sin. How could I even think of disobeying God when he died because of my sin?

This shame-inducing instruction is so oppositional to the actual purpose of Christ's death on the cross. Christ's actions were intended not only to put my sin behavior to death on the cross but my shame feelings as well. Christ's death on the cross was for the specific purpose of ending the bond between sin and shame that was originated by mankind in the Garden of Eden. The sin/shame cycle (sinful behavior leads to shame, driving us to more sin) could only be broken through a radical move on God's part: having his only son die a cruel death on the cross for our salvation.

It is part of my human DNA to feel shame that Jesus had to go as far as death on my behalf for my sins in the first place. In my wildest dreams, I cannot imagine making myself become shame-free, especially for causing someone to die. Fortunately, God did not intend for me to free myself from this awful shame. God designed a sensory side to my brain so I can make the simple choice to focus my five senses on him. This sensory focus is how God frees me from shame. Certainly, the logical side of my brain can't think or reason my way out of this feeling of shame. Human analysis of our faults only induces greater shame. Only through giving up on my own thinking efforts and abilities, and simply looking into Christ's loving eyes, can I feel and embrace God's supernatural, unconditional love. Only feeling his love deep in my bones through sensory focus overcomes and binds my shame.

At the heart of a shamed-filled life is mankind's notoriously headstrong belief in self-driven change and overcoming shame with human effort. Every one of us has a shame story that begins very early in life. As we grow older and chapters are added to this story, many of us go to great length and effort to rewrite or alter our shame story. Unfortunately, our human efforts only result in misery and distortions in our alterations. These attempts at self-alteration only bring on more shame. We desperately try over and over again to change to make ourselves worthy of God's love. Yet nothing can make us worthy and there is nothing we can do can remove our shame. *The Message* says in Isaiah 64:6 that: "We're all sin-infected, sin contaminated. Our best efforts are grease-stained rags." Our personal efforts are utterly useless. Only experiencing God's love through sensory focus lifts our shame.

David in the Bible knew that he could not overcome his own shame. He also knew that sensory focus on God was his only hope. He begged God in *The Message* in Psalms 28:1, "don't turn a deaf ear when I call you, God. If all I get from you is deafening silence, I'd be better off in the Black Hole." In this verse, David is saying that he cannot take care of himself and would rather be obliterated than suffer in shame. David went on to tell God in Psalms 28:2-4, "I'm letting you know what I need, calling out for help and lifting my arms toward your inner sanctum. Don't shove me into the same jail cell with those crooks, with those who are full-time employees of evil. They talk a good line of 'peace', then moonlight for the devil" (*The Message*).

In verses 2-4, David refers to his shame as a jail cell and begs God to remember that David's only way of escape is by calling out to God for help and lifting his arms toward

71

him. A little later on in verses 6-7, David announces that his approach of calling out and reaching up to God has actually worked: "Blessed be God—he heard me praying. He proved he's on my side; I've thrown my lot in with him. Now I'm jumping for joy, and shouting and singing my thanks to him" (*The Message).* In these verses, David expresses his delight over being free from shame and not having to throw himself in a dark hole or be shoved into a jail cell.

I can only stay out of the prison of shame for as long as I keep my sensory focus fixed on Christ. As soon as I look back down at myself, I start to sink again into my miserable feelings of shame. *The Message* describes a very clear picture of what happens when we take our eyes off Jesus. In Matthew 14:28-31, the twelve disciples witness Jesus walking on the water. "Peter, suddenly bold, said, 'Master, if it's really you, call me to come to you on the water.' He said, 'Come ahead.' Jumping out of the boat, Peter walked on the water to Jesus. But when he looked down at the waves churning beneath his feet, he lost his nerve and started to sink. He cried, 'Master, save me!' Jesus didn't hesitate. He reached down and grabbed his hand."

Sensory focus is faith in action and is a very fluid process, just like Peter walking on water. Despite the teaching that Christ died for our sins once and for all, a one-time attempt at sensory focus on Christ is not a magic pill that frees me from shame once and for all. Christ only had to die once to show that his love is unconditional, but sensory focus was designed to be continual, not a one-time deal. As soon as Peter looked down, he began to sink. When I take my sensory focus off God, my shame automatically reappears and will lead me to sin again. Only if I choose to let any jolt of shame quickly drive me back to my sensory focus on Christ, can the sin/shame cycle stay in remission. To me it is genius on God's part, to free me of shame and then use it to remind me to put my sensory attention back on him when my shame wiggles its way back into my field of vision. If anything is a red flag and a big bold reminder to run back to sensory focus on God, it's my poor, pitiful shame.

Peter walking on water is a spectacular example of what happens when we put our sensory focus on God. What stands out to me about this story, even more Peter walking on water, is what happened when he took his eyes off Jesus. The split second Peter looked down, he began to sink. The sensation of sinking affected his sensory brain instantaneously, and he immediately cried out to God to save him. Just as quickly, without hesitation, Jesus grabbed onto him. There was no time for Peter to hang his head in shame for taking his eyes of Jesus. Jesus wasted no time in grabbing Peter's hand. He did not shame Peter before he rescued him. This dynamic of quickly crying out to God and God grabbing onto us is how the shame factor stays in remission.

The shame factor that has produced performance-based cultures and churches down through the ages has also been the driving force in earthly human addictions. Ask alcoholics if shame kept them from drinking again or if shame triggered their next alcoholic episode—I guarantee they will tell you shame is a serious trigger for relapse. The sin/shame cycle is remarkably similar to the addiction/shame cycle. Whether it's our own thinking or performance addiction, or the vast, endless variety of other earthly addictions, shame is the catalyst or common denominator for every addiction known to man. Only heavenly addiction is shame-free.

Just as I never understood God's brilliant design of sensory focus in our brain, I never understood his incredible plan to carry not only our sin, but our feeling of shame as well. That is what heavenly addiction is all about. When I made the choice to focus rather than perform, God gave me a whole new lease on life, which includes the feeling of complete freedom from shame. I now am totally immersed in the feeling Jesus describes in Matthew 11:30: "For my yoke is easy and my burden is light" (NIV). Sensory focus on Jesus is easy—human performance is hard. The feeling of being stuck in my own shame is so heavy, but God carrying my shame makes me feel as light as a cloud.

Why would any of us want to pass up a new life that is easy and light? In my own case, I passed it up until about four years ago simply out of ignorance. I never read the Bible closely or really studied the brain. These new sources of knowledge have revolutionized my life and brought me such freedom.

Previously, my whole life was all about shame. I was told as early as I can remember that I was difficult to love. My shame story began in preschool and grew into many volumes over the next five decades until my whole identity was permeated with shame. Shame infiltrated my career and relationships, personal and professional. My shame blocked a loving relationship with God and others. Shame not only blocked any freedom to love but also freedom to feel anger or hurt.

Shame can build and become so pervasive in our lives that we allow shame to essentially block the use of the sensory side of our brain. Along with this sensory blockage, our range of emotions that include joy, anger, love and hurt are submerged in our subconscious self as well. I do counseling with clients who are so suppressed and feel so shut-down in life that they do not even experience the taste of the food they eat or enjoy the fresh air that they breathe. These clients and many other people have deteriorated emotionally to the degree where they are held hostage by their own efforts to break out of their shame.

On my own efforts, it was futile to overcome my own shame. Since I was never taught that only Christ can overcome my shame, I was forever trying desperately to bust out of my emotional prison. I felt I was living out two life sentences: one in the mental prison of my thoughts and another in the emotional prison of my feelings. I could have never have imagined that God could—let alone would—break down the mental and emotional prison walls simply through the choice to give him my sensory focus. I was so desperate that, even in my shame, just for a moment I stopped looking down and hanging my head. As soon as I looked up at him, he looked back at me with such an intense love that, in that moment, I experienced a moment of freedom from my shame.

Since I looked up that first time, I have looked down again many times at my shame, simply out of human habit. I automatically hang my head for a little bit, but I now hate my shame so much, I make the conscious choice to look back up at him. He is always faithful to look back at me with his caring eyes. He never shames me for my shame, he always has that compassionate look of empathy that says he knows how awful shame feels and longs to rescue me from that terrible feeling. When I share my personal experience with clients, they respond that it is so hard to stop hanging their head in shame. I simply teach them that the difficulty lies in our subconscious where we naturally hang our heads out of human conditioning. Lifting our heads is not physically difficult and does not require any performance effort, just the conscious choice to look at God. His loving look back at us is the secret to lifting our feeling of shame.

During the past four years, God has shown me the definition of sensory discipline. Unlike the typical definition of discipline, sensory discipline is a discipline of choice, not effort. Mistakenly, I used to believe that sensory focus required effort because it was so hard. I constantly reverted back to my thinking brain rather than dwelling in my sensory brain. I was always thinking about things rather than living in the moment with my five senses. I did not realize that my brain was programmed or conditioned to be in the thinking mode rather than the sensory mode. I subconsciously operated in the thinking mode, which seems natural for those of us who are performance-driven over-achievers. We are hard-wired to run our own lives with a vigilance that keeps us hyper-attentive to what we are thinking.

With my brain preset in the thought mode, my only way of escaping from myself and allowing God to run my life is a continual, conscious choice to switch to my sensory brain by giving him the attention of my five senses. While it seemed so hard to think about choosing sensory focus, the simplicity and ease of this practice has been shocking to me. All I needed to do was stop thinking and just do it. For example, through a simple choice, without any human effort at all, I can turn my head to alter my visual attention. I can walk to a different location for a change in sounds or smells. I can move my hands for a different touch. I can change what I put in my mouth for a different taste.

Compared to the difficulty of changing my thoughts and mental discipline, changing the direction of my five senses is so simple, even though I still have to make a conscious choice to override my natural tendency to dwell in my thinking brain. These continual conscious choices to stay in the sensory realm (sensory discipline) bring me so much freedom from my naturally negative thinking, and from the anxiety that is bound to my thoughts. These conscious choices to practice sensory focus also free my thinking brain to receive the endless supply of thoughts that God implants into my logical brain. This sets the pattern for allowing God to run my life, rather than letting my own distorted, negative thought-patterns govern my daily behavior.

For me, it all boils down to the simple, conscious choice to switch from cognitive focus to sensory focus. Although it has always made "sense" to me that I was hard-wired for cognitive sensibility, my human conditioning only kept me forever trapped in my shame, which has always resulted in a trip to the triple-A club: anxiety, anger and addiction. Even worse, after a period of time at the triple-A club, I always end up with a massive depression hangover.

This negative outcome was rooted in my ongoing, oppressive story of shame and self-condemnation, which provided a constant flow of background noise that kept me trapped in my head while I tried to conduct normal life activities each and every day. My thoughts could get quite speculative and distorted. This automatic shame-filled thought-stream formed a self-protective defense mechanism to shield me from any sudden surprise or shock attack. The huge reservoir of behaviors that made constant deposits into my shame bank left me living in constant fear of some catastrophic, haunting end-result, where I would be doomed forever, the laughingstock of everyone in my life.

For many years, my life operated in shame just below the radar screen of any level of conscious awareness on my part. No one ever taught me that life was all about the shame unless I gave my sensory focus to God. In fact, my vast reservoir of shameful feelings occupied the sensory side of my brain, leaving me blinded from the light of God's intense love. Since shame represents the sensory side of sin, it is the blocking agent to experience God's love with our five senses. I am so grateful that my shame brought me to such a dismal conclusion that I was moved by God to look up for a moment so Christ could embrace me with the depth of his love.

Without God's love giving us the power to embrace a shame-free life, mankind is doomed to a lifetime of earthy addictions. In fact, shame is the energy supply for every addiction in the shame/addiction cycle. Our only hope is a sensory focus on God rather than a sensory focus on earthly addictions, so he can flush out our shame. Our shame is not eradicated by the mere cognitive knowledge that God loves us, but through the moment-to-moment sensory experience of his love that happens only when we devote the attention of our five senses to him.

This sensory devotion is how God overpowers our shame with his love. Staying in his presence and experiencing him with our five senses all day long is our only safeguard against our shame rushing back in. When I stumble onto pockets of old shame lodged in the unconscious recesses of my brain, I quickly run to God with the elevated attention of my five senses, through which he so graciously allows me to experience his absolution in a sensory way. It is only when I rush into his presence under the umbrella of his love that I feel free from shame. Otherwise, in my shame, I will end up in disobedience again as I desperately attempt to escape my shame through my own futile efforts and addictive escapes.

"I'm single-minded in pursuit of you; don't let me miss the road signs you've posted. I've banked your promises in the vault of my heart so I won't sin myself bankrupt. Be blessed, God; train me in your ways of wise living. I'll transfer to my lips all the counsel that comes from your mouth; I delight far more in what you tell me about living than in gathering a pile of riches. I ponder every morsel of wisdom from you, I attentively watch how you've done it. I relish everything you've told me of life, I won't forget a word of it. Be generous with me and I'll live a full life; not for a minute will I take my eyes off your road" (Psalm 119:10-1, *The Message*).

Chapter Five

The Bible and the Brain

"If you're a hard worker and do a good job, you deserve your pay; we don't call your wages a gift. But if you see that the job is too big for you, that it's something only God can do, and you trust Him to do it—you could never do it yourself no matter how hard and how long you worked—well, that trusting-him-to-do-it is what gets you set right with God, by God. Sheer gift. David confirms this way of looking at it, saying that the one who trusts God to do the putting-everything-right without insisting on having a say in it is one fortunate man."

- Romans 4:4-8, *The Message*

Our culture engrains in our minds from an early age that the only person we can really depend on is ourselves. As children, we hear phrases like "Never give up on yourself" or "If you fall, pick yourself back up again!" With that backdrop, you might be wondering why anyone, especially a counselor, would ever encourage anyone to quit or give up on themselves. It seems so counterintuitive to say it is a good thing to quit on yourself! In fact, giving up on yourself feels like a kind of betrayal.

And that's the whole problem. Our core cultural belief in ourselves goes directly against the instructions of God. He desperately desires for us to give up on ourselves. This does not mean that he wants us to end our lives—he simply wants us to stop trying to self-govern. He knows what a disaster we make of things when we try to run our own lives. He sees the self-driven, shame-filled life we end up stuck in time and time again.

Again, our culture instills in us a core belief that it is essential to think for ourselves. We can't stop trying to self-govern unless we let God take over our thought life and allow him to do all our thinking for us.

When I share this teaching with others, almost everyone is shocked by this seemingly radical concept. The truth is that this concept of allowing God to think for us is not my own idea. This teaching comes directly out of God's Word—it only seems like a foreign idea because it goes so directly against our natural inclinations that every culture down through the ages has tried to drown out its voice. This idea continues to seem so strange to us in spite of excellent examples in the Bible like Paul, who was Saul before God took over his life.

Saul, without a doubt, was running his own show when he was killing Jews for an occupation. It took God striking him blind on the road to Damascus before Saul understood who was really in charge. Because of his radical conversion where Saul became Paul, there was never any debate about the impact of God's governance on the rest of Paul's life. Paul totally embraced God running his life and never wanted to turn back. What a brilliant example of how God turns our lives upside down when we simply choose to let him take over! The results of God running our lives are as breathtaking as the impact God had on Paul's life.

Perhaps the most breathtaking of all is the simplicity of God's masterplan to run our lives. When we make our futile attempts to run our own lives, we feel bombarded by so many choices that we can get completely overwhelmed by decisions that we have to make. When we accept God's invitation to live under his rule, he only asks us to make one simple choice. This simple choice is to give him the attention of our five senses. While some would argue that this choice is too difficult, that is simply not true. God designed our brains with the ability to give him our sensory focus without any mental effort whatsoever. His brain design for each of us requires no need to perform at all. God knew that if his design required any self-performance on our part, we would take our eyes off him. In his magnificent wisdom God made the choice to put our sensory focus on him as easy as walking into a kitchen and experiencing the sweet aroma of chocolate chip cookies. We don't need to put any performance effort whatsoever in smelling the cookies. Without trying at all, the sweet aroma of the cookies invades our sense of smell.

This one simple choice to give God the attention of our five senses has a lot of common ground with the attachment bond theory described by Segal and Jaffe that was highlighted in the previous chapter. This theory described the first interactive love relationship of the infant with their primary caregiver, typically the mother. Since the infant is too young to express their attachment verbally, this is simply a sensory experience for them as they emotionally attach to their primary caregiver (Segal and Jaffe, 2016). Segal and Jaffe emphasize that this initial attachment bond shapes the infant's brain, profoundly influencing their self-esteem (2016). Since God is the designer of the human brain, our brain has the same capacity to attach to him in a sensory manner just as the infant can attach to their primary caregiver.

God's simple plan for our entire lives is to be our spiritual primary care giver. In the Bible, God says he wants us to come to him as little children. There are multiple scriptures that spell out this plan. *The Message* says, in Matthew 18:2-5, "For an answer Jesus called over a child, whom he stood in the middle of the room, and said, 'I'm telling you, once and for all, unless you return to square one and start over like children, you're not even going to get a look at the kingdom, let alone get in. Whoever becomes simple and elemental again, like this child, will rank high in God's kingdom.'" Jesus's command to become "simple and elemental" refers to learning to live in the moment, tuned-in to our five senses, like a small child lives.

Another scripture that spells out God's simple plan to be our spiritual primary caregiver is found in *The Message* in Luke 18:15-17 where it says, "People brought babies to Jesus, hoping he might touch them. When the disciples saw it, they shooed them off. Jesus called them back. 'Let these children alone. Don't get between them and me. These children are the kingdom's pride and joy. Mark this: Unless you accept God's kingdom in the simplicity of a child, you'll never get in.'"

Basically, Jesus told his disciples very bluntly not to come between God and anyone who simply gives him their total sensory attention like a child would. Sensory attachment to God is the secret to experiencing a close loving relationship with him. As Segal and Jaffe (2016) specified in their writing on the infant attachment bond, a sensory emotional based connection is what shapes our brain into being able to experience secure, loving relationships in life.

Just as infants are totally dependent on the primary caregiver for this secure loving attachment, those of us who are God's children are completely dependent on him for a secure spiritual attachment. *The Message* says in Psalm

131:2 that David's relationship with God was "Like a baby content in its mother's arms." *The Message* also says in Psalm 31:23 that "God takes care of all those who stay close to him." Just like little children who constantly hang onto their mother's skirt, we hang onto God continually with all of our five senses. We want to hear his voice, never let him out of our sight, smell him, taste him and touch him. *The Message* goes onto report in Psalm 91:14-16 that God says: "If you'll hold onto me for dear life . . . I'll get you out of trouble, I'll give you the best of care if you'll only get to know and trust me. Call me and I'll answer, be at your side in bad times; I'll rescue you, then throw you a party."

Somehow, down through the ages, we have totally missed the simplicity of God's plan for our lives. We have not only made trusting in God a huge mental performance exercise, but we have also made even the *experience* of feeling close to him into an achievement that takes effort. We have missed God's simplicity in spite of scriptures like Proverbs 3:5 (NKJV), where the Bible says, "Trust in The Lord with all your heart, and lean not on your own understanding." Giving the Lord the total attention of our five senses is how we put this trust into action. This is how we trust "with all our heart." Trust has nothing to do with our thinking. In fact, thinking and trying to figure things out for ourselves totally gets in the way of putting our trust in God. Our own thinking only draws our focus to ourselves and away from God.

God wanted to give us a way of escape from our own thinking, so he designed our brains and nervous systems in a manner that allows us to escape our own thoughts. This escape occurs when we focus on him with our five senses. Our brain has special cells called neurons that handle sensory input. When our sensory neurons receive information from our eyes or ears, nose or mouth, or from any of the many, many nerve endings in our skin, they relay messages to each other, creating connections known as neural pathways. Over time, those neural pathways are what help create patterns in how we think and act. In fact, the more certain pathways are used, the easier and easier it is for us to behave in certain ways or think certain things.

As a result, when we choose to give God the attention of these five senses, he ends up determining the way we think, learn, move, and behave. When our sensory focus is on God, our mind is emptied of our own thoughts and refilled with God's thoughts so we can lean on his understanding. This one simple choice on our part puts God in charge of the rest of the process and makes us dependent on him. When we keep our sensory focus on him (which is what the phrase "praying without ceasing" actually means), God directs this repetitive neuron travel, so that living in his reality becomes easier and easier. As we maintain our sensory dependency on him, God continually shapes our identity to transform our lives into something better.

Why would God want our brains to be receptors for his thoughts and not dependent on our own thoughts? He answers this question in Psalms 55:8-11 where *The Message* says "I don't think the way you think. The way you work isn't the way I work. . . For as the sky soars high above earth, so the way I work surpasses the way you work, and the way I think is beyond the way you think." God wants something way better for us than our own thinking. That's how much he loves us. In Proverbs 3:6 (NKJV), the Bible goes on to say, "in all your ways acknowledge him and he shall direct your paths." The

Hebrew word for "acknowledge" means to experience or know with your heart, not your head, and can even mean to "devour." In other words, our thoughts are not the means by which we acknowledge God. We acknowledge God by experiencing him with our five senses. This reminds me of the time I visited a Krispy Kreme, where they make donuts right in front of you. I could see, smell, taste and touch those donuts, and you better believe that all that sensory input gave me a powerful desire to devour them!

This is how God brilliantly designed our brains with the capacity to totally devour him with our five senses, so that we want nothing more than to depend on him to run our lives. He invites us to let him run our lives and even says he will do it as a gift, free of charge. When God created man, he never intended for him to run his own life. God knew that thinking for ourselves would only make us an anxious mess. He specifically designed our brains so only his thoughts would lead us to a wonderful life. Any attempt we make through our own efforts will always result in anxiety, earthly addictions, and other self-defeating behavior. Not that God enjoys watching us suffer through our failures. He suffers with us when we hold back from letting him take care of us like only he knows how.

Why then is man so persistent in running his own life? I only know how to answer that question from my own life experience. To make a long, sad story short, I have always read in scripture that God wanted to run my life. The scripture repeatedly spells out that instruction. My problem was that I never really searched the scriptures deeply enough so God could show me "how" to let him run my life. In addition, I never learned how God designed the brain in such a way that would show me how he created me so he could run my life. My "ignorance" of the Bible and the brain held me back from God's revelation on how it works for him to run my life each minute of every day.

I believe millions of people in many cultures and many churches are living in the same ignorance I lived in until a few years ago. Ever since I learned how God intended to run my life, he has radically transformed my entire being. I simply want to share this transformation with everyone who will read "Heavenly Addiction." I also wrote my previous book, "Clear My Vision," as a devotional intended to provide many more scriptures that are the biblical foundation for "Heavenly Addiction." Despite how radically different my writing is from mainstream teaching on how to live a successful life, I trust God and his Word will transform your life in the same way he transformed my life in the past few years.

What *The Message* says in Isaiah 46:3-4 is confirmation of my trust in God and his Word to transform me: "Listen to me, family of Jacob, everyone that's left of the family of Israel. I've been carrying you on my back from the day you were born, and I'll keep on carrying you when you're old. I'll be there, bearing you when you're old and gray. I've done it and will keep on doing it, carrying you on my back, saving you." Later on in Isaiah 46:9-11, *The Message* provides additional confirmation:

"I am God, the only God you've ever had or ever will have—incomparable, irreplaceable—From the very beginning telling you what the ending will be, All along letting you in on what is going to happen, Assuring you, 'I'm in this for the long haul, I'll do exactly what I set out to do,' Calling that eagle, Cyrus, out of the east, from a far country the man I chose to help me. I've said it, and I'll certainly do it. I've planned it, so it's as good as done."

Learning about the term "sensory focus" is the missing link to understanding the process God uses to think on our behalf and to run our lives. Giving God the attention of our five senses is not nearly as difficult to do as many people think it is. It is simply being in God's presence and experiencing him in the moment through some or all of our five senses. What does it look like to be in God's presence? The great news is that we are already in his presence because God is everywhere. In Psalm 139:7-12, King David asks God, "Is there any place I can go to avoid your Spirit? To be out of your sight? If I climb to the sky, you're there! If I go underground, you're there! If I flew on morning's wings to the far western horizon, you'd find me in a minute—you're already there waiting! Then I said to myself, 'Oh, he even sees me in the dark! At night I'm immersed in the light!' It's a fact: darkness isn't dark to you; night and day, darkness and light, they're all the same to you" (*The Message*).

Because God is already everywhere, he never needs to go anywhere. He is always near as he says in *The Message* (Jeremiah 23:23-24): "Am I not a God near at hand . . . and not a God far off? Can anyone hide out in a corner where I can't see him? . . . Am I not present everywhere, whether seen or unseen?" God is never out of our sensory reach. We can sense his presence even in the dark. He is literally omnipresent—present all around us. Not only that—we cannot move or even exist without him! In Acts 17:28, *The Message* says, "We live and move in him, can't get away from him."

If God loves us so much that we can't get away from him, then how has our culture and church managed to operate down through the ages as if it is such a great struggle to closely attach to him? Despite the reality that

God lives and moves in us, we can totally miss this continual intense sensory connection to him by devoting our sensory attention to earthly addictions. Our earthly addictions are activated by thinking for ourselves and believing we can run our own lives. We are blinded from seeing God by dwelling on our own thoughts, which are so distorted they often delude us into thinking that we can make it successfully through life with our own wisdom. This self-centered mentality always leads us down the highway to the dead end of self-destruction.

God's creation of the Garden of Eden was to provide Adam and Eve with an ideal environment that would captivate their sensory brains. He wanted them to continually dwell in the sensory side of their brain with him so that their thinking side was simply a receptor for his thoughts. He never intended for Adam and Eve or the rest of mankind to think for themselves. Satan lured Eve into thinking for herself and Adam joined her. *The Message* says in Genesis 3:4-6, "The serpent told the Woman, 'You won't die. God knows that the moment you eat from the tree, you'll see what's really going on. You'll be just like God, knowing everything, ranging all the way from good to evil.' When the Woman saw that the tree looked like good eating and realized what she would get out of it—she'd know everything!—she took and ate the fruit and then gave some to her husband and he ate."

Adam and Eve set the pattern for the rest of mankind to be distracted from God's original plan for creation. Since the beginning, everyone's automatic inclination is to focus on their own thinking and not follow God's master plan of focusing on him through our five senses. Everyone's natural tendency is to try to be just like God, wanting to be wise and know everything ourselves, instead of simply wanting to be dependent on him for everything.

This human inclination to try to compete with God and be independent in our thinking is why our culture and church have essentially bypassed the sensory side of the brain and given all the attention to the thinking side of the brain. When the sensory side is ignored, the thinking side is naturally self-focused, because the God who surrounds us and whose spirit resides in our heart is going unnoticed. It is impossible to let God run our lives when we don't notice him, because he doesn't have the attention of our five senses or our heart. Even though God made it so simple to give him our sensory attention, we completely miss his plan out of our ignorance of the Bible and the brain.

Fortunately, God overlooks our ignorance when no one has enlightened us to God's truth. In Acts 17:30-3, *The Message* says "God overlooks it as long as you don't know any better—but that time is past. The unknown is now known, and he's calling for a radical life change." I know for sure I lived in ignorance for many, many years. Thankfully, I was finally enlightened to God's truth. I now feel compelled by God's endless love to share this enlightenment with everyone I can for the rest of my years here on earth. Sensory focus on God throughout my day brings me joy beyond what I could have ever imagined. My eyes are wide open to the reality that I have only begun to experience the many benefits of this teaching on sensory focus. However, I write with the full knowledge that billions of people are still suffering in ignorance.

With our society, homes, schools, churches, jobs and even sports putting all the emphasis on our thinking brain, it is not surprising that the sensory side gets ignored. Schools and sports are starting to use the word "focus" more frequently, but they typically use the word in the context of thinking and continue to ignore sensory focus. People everywhere are still taught from an early age to depend on their own thinking and reasoning abilities. Everyone takes for granted that their brain is to be utilized to analyze life and to figure out and solve their own problems. When the brain is utilized in this way, people become totally dependent on themselves and their own thinking to run their daily lives. They experience atrophy in their use of the sensory brain and focus on God seems unnatural and out of character. No wonder so many of us have been clueless about how to focus on God. No wonder "focus" is still the missing word in our vocabulary. No wonder so many of us have spent most of our lives an anxious mess, chasing one earthly addiction or another.

No wonder it takes feeling tortured in our own mental prisons to clearly show us that self-focus results in disaster! Reaching the end of ourselves is a necessary prerequisite to being ready and willing to let God run our lives.

Part of the genius of how God designed the brain is that he will not allow the thinking side of our brain to atrophy while we remain in his presence on the sensory side of our brain. It is true that sensory focus on God will empty our thinking mind of our own thoughts. A huge aspect of sensory focus on God and not self is the reduction of worry and anxiety in that thinking space as well. However, just because we are not anxious or worried does not mean that side of our brain is left empty! God has an endless supply of his thoughts to fill that empty space. He fills our thinking center with his thoughts, his analysis, his solutions. He takes us into his reality and we live with him, even while we are still located on this earth.

At this defining juncture in our lives, where we quit on ourselves and finally want to belong to God, the mystery that remains is exactly how, in a step-by-step manner, do we live in continual total sensory dependence on God? How does that translate into practical, everyday living? With the attention of our five senses fixed on God, how exactly does he run our lives? How does he empty our minds of anxious negativistic thinking and fill the logical center of our brains with his thoughts? How does God "put a little of Heaven in our hearts so that we'll never settle for less?" (2 Corinthians 5:5, *The Message*).

Now we must ask the question: how does God's love move us "to such extremes" that his love "has the first and last word in everything we do" so that we are living in God's reality for the remainder of our time here on earth? (2 Corinthians 5:14 *The Message*).

"I've called your name. You're mine. When you're in over your head, I'll be there with you. When you're in rough waters, you will not go down. When you're between a rock and a hard place, it won't be a dead end—Because I am your God, your personal God, The Holy God of Israel, your Savior" (Isaiah 43:2-3, *The Message*).

Chapter Six

The Choice for Sensory Focus

"Everyone who confesses that Jesus is God's Son participates continuously in an intimate relationship with God. We know it so well, we've embraced it heart and soul, this love that comes from God."

- 1 John 4:15-16, *The Message*

From a human thinking perspective, it is impossible to participate continuously in an intimate relationship with God. It would take an incredible effort on our part to concentrate our thoughts on him all day long and we would still end up in utter failure. Since human beings have anywhere from 40,000 to 70,000 thoughts a day, everyone would fall over from sheer exhaustion if they tried only to think about God! Yet, many people, including church leaders, ignorantly believe that a perfect relationship with God requires this level of devotion in our thought life. Many people totally evaluate themselves based on how they are performing in their thought life with God and how well they are obeying God. While this approach to our relationship with God resembles what happens in almost everyone's mind, these two measures of evaluating ourselves are bad habits taught by our culture and church that look nothing like what God actually had in mind for our relationship with him.

What God had in mind for our relationship with him is clearly spelled out Psalm 27:4-5 (*The Message*) where David writes, ". . . To live with him in his house my whole life long. I'll contemplate his beauty; I'll study at his feet. That's the only quiet, secure place in a noisy world, the perfect getaway, far from the buzz of traffic." The word here translated "contemplate" comes from the Hebrew "to gaze," which refers to our sensory mind, not our thinking mind. An admiring gaze perfectly captures the attitude David was describing in this Psalm. David's admiration for God's beauty took him to his quiet, perfect getaway. He describes another beautiful picture of what God desires in our relationship with him in Psalm 71:22-24, where he writes, "And I'll take up the lute and thank you to the tune of your faithfulness, God. I'll make music for you on a harp, Holy One of Israel. When I open up in song to you, I let out lungs full of praise, my rescued life a song. All day long I'm chanting about you . . ." (*The Message*).

While it is humanly impossible to think about God all day long, God miraculously created our brain so we would have the capacity to devote our five senses to him on a continual basis: ("embrace it heart and soul"). God, in his genius, created a sensory side of our brain that has the capacity to continually focus on him, even though this is impossible with our thinking mind. Our sensory brain can be in full focus-on-God mode before our thoughts are even formed. In his brilliance, God structured our brain so that when we maintain our sensory focus on him, God is in charge of the thoughts that are formed from the input of our five senses. For example, when we immerse our senses on chocolate chip cookies, we smell them before we label the smell with our thoughts. When we have our senses on God, he labels what we are sensing with his thoughts.

God designed our brain to experience him in exactly the same way that we experience the smell of cookies. When we confess him as our only hope to live life, God invades our five senses with his presence and a love that we can only feel when he has our undivided sensory attention. We simply choose, without having to try, to give him our total sensory focus. Just like David, by giving God the attention of our five senses, we experience the perfect getaway without having to travel to the mountains or the beach. There is no human effort involved, the same way there is no effort to smell the cookies. God has filled our heart and soul with his love, and he surrounds us with his sweet aroma to make it impossible to miss him when our sensory attention is centered on him. Since God is already everywhere and omnipresent, all we have to do is choose to engage with God in the moment with our five senses.

One would think it would be virtually impossible to miss this sensory engagement with God. After all, would any of us miss the smell of cookies baking while standing in the kitchen in the presence of their sweet aroma? How can we possibly miss God with our five senses if he is all around us and even lives in us? It seems like feeling close to God with our sensory attention should be the most natural, automatic engagement on the planet. After all, that was God's original design for the Garden of Eden. Yet, so quickly and easily, Adam and Eve made the simple choice to take their sensory focus off God by the action of thinking for themselves.

Just like with Adam and Eve, we all have attractive-looking distractions that can influence our choice to focus our senses on God. For example, what about when we walk into the local 7-11 store, pick up a snack to eat, and then stop at the cash register to pay, only to be distracted by the sexy magazines deliberately positioned at eye level? It can be so easy to gaze at these magazines without even intending to look. Fortunately, God also gave us four other senses and we can simply choose to have praise music in our ears to focus on, instead of the sexy magazines. Like many of us, I was ignorant of these sensory alternatives to the visual until God showed me during my study of the Bible and the brain.

Part of God's masterplan for mankind was freedom of choice. He creates all of us with the same freedom of choice that he originally gave Adam and Eve. Down through the ages, all of us have followed in Adam and Eve's footsteps, making the choice to think for ourselves rather than remain in the moment focused on God with our five senses. What God created to be a very natural experience, man has made to seem unnatural. We have all been so indoctrinated to think for ourselves that this thinking has conditioned us not to naturally just dwell in the moment with our five senses enjoying the presence of God. We are all so pre-programmed to be thinking all the time that moment-by-moment sensory focus choices seem foreign to us. The church in many cases has perpetuated this programming by emphasizing that our relationship with God is an intellectual experience, rather than a sensory relationship. God designed this sensory relationship for the specific purpose of giving us the freedom of choice to give our sensory focus to him and not anything that would harm us.

This intellectual programming is done out of total ignorance, because we have not embraced the true meaning of God's Word, and have not taken the time to learn how God created our brains. The Bible is so clear how God designed our relationship with him to be a sensory connection. Psalms is the longest book in the Bible, and this book repeats over and over again in every chapter the example of David and his sensory attachment to God.

When David says in the Bible, "When I open up in song to you," he is opening up his senses to God through song. This is reflective of how brilliantly God created our brain with a design that makes it possible through sensory devotion to spend intimate time with God all day long: "All day long I'm chanting about you." Chanting is not thinking, it is repetitive, rhythmic sensory sounds that require no mental effort. God made our brains in such a fashion that we can simply choose to get away with him continuously by directing our sensory attention to him. This continual choice empties the thinking side of our brain of worries, of struggle, of analysis, of performance and allows God to perform in us while we cling to him. While this is counter-intuitive to the messages we have absorbed over the years, the choice to focus our senses on him is clear instruction directly out of God's word.

Throughout Psalm 119 in *The Message*, there are examples over and over again of this clear instruction for sensory focus. Verse 10 says: "I'm single-minded in pursuit of you"—meaning that each one of my five senses are focused on God. Throughout this entire chapter, there are frequent references to these five senses: words like sing, walk, smile, see, dance, hold, tasty, embrace, shiver, speechless. Verse 145 says: "I call out at the top of my lungs" and verse 169 says: "Let my cry come right into your presence, God." These words and phrases are all sensory-driven and so descriptive of how David gave God the attention of all five of his senses.

God showed me a crystal-clear picture of what this constant sensory focus on him looks like. The choice to place our sensory focus on God is fluid. It is a continual, ongoing opportunity. It is like a steady stream of living water where we simply step under the shower of his grace by casting our five senses on him. God's downpour of cleansing water never gets turned off. We may step away from under the water current, but even that interruption is a cold, wet reminder of how good we feel staying directly under his warm, comforting water fall.

Far too many people totally miss out on God's soothing, living waterfall, because they are so fixated on their own thoughts that they completely bypass their sensory brain function. We are culturally programmed to automatically fixate on the daily stresses right in front of us. Through constant worry and our mental struggle to figure out life for ourselves, our sensory signals are not receptive to his presence even though God is directly in our midst. He has not moved away from us at all, but we are too caught up in our own thought-prisons to sense his presence. We are so fixated on ourselves that we do not even notice the water mist blowing our way from the falls. We seem to come by this self-fixation naturally because our culture and churches place such a high premium on knowledge. Yet, this preoccupation to gain more knowledge is not by God's design. As Paul writes in 1 Corinthians 8:1, "while knowledge makes us feel important, it is love that strengthens the church" (NLT).

The spectacular news is that God's clear plan is to highlight love over knowledge. He does this by loving us unconditionally and giving us love for him in return. God carries out this plan through the architecture of our brain when he created us with the ability to quickly shift our brain from puffed up self-thought focus to sensory God focus through the simple choice to turn our senses to him. This sensory focus on God guarantees that loving feeling for him that progressively builds into a heavenly addiction.

Exactly how does this simple choice to shift back to the sensory side work? God created our brain with bridges to take us from the thinking side to the sensory side (no need for each of us to be slave laborers to build underground tunnels of earthly addiction). We can cross these bridges from our thoughts to our five senses through rhythmic sights, sounds, smells, tastes and touch. People everywhere have crossed these bridges for centuries without knowing what was happening in their brains. For example, relaxing on a rocking chair involves rhythmic motion and even sound with the old squeaky rockers. It is possible to override the rhythms with intense thinking; but, through the simple practice of consciously choosing to tune in your sensory signals to the motion, you will quickly cross the bridge to the sensory side away from your thoughts.

I have learned that a great way for me to observe how my brain crosses back and forth between the sensory side and thinking side of the brain is when I play tennis with my younger brother two or three times a week. One of us will bring up a subject to discuss in between games and I have a habit of continuing to think about the subject of conversation when we resume play. Sure enough, I end up misplaying several shots in a row because I am still operating in the thinking side of my brain rather than being in the moment on the sensory side of the brain and watching the ball intently.

The good news is that as soon as it occurs to me that I am still running thoughts through my head, I quickly cross the bridge to the sensory side of my brain and put my full visual focus on the ball. With my full visual focus on the ball, the thinking conversation in my head immediately goes away. It is amazing to me how God designed our brains so that sensory focus turns our brain off to our own thoughts. As a bonus, I go back to hitting the tennis ball really well because I have my complete visual focus back on the ball. As an added bonus, tennis always has brief breaks in-between serves. I use these momentary interludes to remind myself to watch the ball continuously from the moment my brother tosses it in the air to serve until the ball hits off my racquet as I return the shot.

A sports reporter supposedly asked a highly successful tennis pro the secret to his success. The tennis player quickly responded: "I focus on watching the ball." The reporter quickly responded back to the player, "everyone does that." The reporter, like most people, took sensory focus for granted. One might think it would be natural to watch the ball without constant reminders but, for most people, the only thing that seems natural is thinking—not sensory focus.

Since the original sin of Adam and Eve, we have all been cursed with the natural tendency to think on our own. We automatically operate in the thinking side of our brain, bypassing the side of our brain that God designed for the specific purpose of operating in the sensory realm with the focus of our senses on him. Since the original sin of Adam and Eve, we no longer naturally dwell in God's presence. Only God can re-generate us and free us from ourselves to able to dwell in his presence with our five senses as he originally created us.

God offers us this re-generation and freedom through Christ's death and resurrection on the cross. This ultimate sacrifice of his son gave every one of us the opportunity to begin anew our sensory focus on him and be freed from our slavery to sin and our natural tendency to live in the mental prison of our own thinking. This opportunity to get a fresh start in life is clearly spelled out in *The Message*, 2 Corinthians 14-15: "Our firm decision is to work from this focused center: One man died for everyone. That puts everyone in the same boat. He included everyone in his death so that everyone could be included in his life, a resurrection life, a far better life than people ever lived on their own."

The Message in 2 Corinthians 5 goes on to say in verses 16-17, "Because of this decision we don't evaluate people by what they have or how they look. We looked at the Messiah that way once and got it all wrong, as you know. We certainly don't look at him that way anymore. Now we look inside, and what we see is that anyone united with the Messiah gets a fresh start, is created new. The old life is gone; a new life burgeons."

When people are initially exposed to my teaching on this new "FocusChoice Life," they often do not immediately experience the simplicity of the instructions on how to give God the continual attention of their five senses. People often comment how hard it is. It seems hard, but not because sensory focus is difficult. Sensory focus does not demand any performance effort at all, it only requires the simple choice to shift the attention of our brain to the sensory side by focusing on one or more of our five senses of sight, smell, sound, taste and touch. It requires no effort or struggle to smell, see, hear, taste or touch. They are simple choices we make.

What make these simple choices seem so difficult is our natural resistance from our years and years of false teaching and the bad habit we practiced year after year of self-thinking. We have such ingrained, strong cultural and church indoctrination and traditions of thinking for ourselves that sensory focus on God seems virtually impossible and completely foreign and unnatural. It feels very much like the discomfort of eating meals with the wrong hand.

Despite the fact that our culture and our church resist God's simple teaching on sensory focus, the secret to a free life lies in what we choose to focus on. What we focus on drives our life. When we give our sensory attention to God, he drives our life. In a way, we willingly become his slave. Yet, it is this total dependency on him that sets us free. He sets us free from self-focus and the mental prison that results from driving our own lives. Even the disciples had a difficult time with this teaching on sensory focus, in spite of the reality that Christ was physically in their presence. *The Message* in John 6:60 says that "Many among the disciples heard this and said, 'This is tough teaching, too tough to swallow.'" *The Message* goes on to say in the same chapter in John in verses 63-65 that "Sheer muscle and willpower don't make anything happen. . . This is why I told you earlier that no one is capable of coming to me on his own. You get to me only as a gift from the Father."

In other words, God's design of the brain so that we are able to continually keep our focus on him is a gift, not something that we can achieve through any herculean amount of human effort. *The Message* in 1 Peter 1:13-16 also describes this focus of the sensory mind as a gift: "So roll up your sleeves, put your mind in gear, be totally ready to receive the gift that's coming when Jesus arrives. Don't lazily slip back into those old grooves of evil, doing just what you feel like doing. You didn't know any better then; you do now. As obedient children, let yourselves be pulled into a way of life shaped by God's life, a life energetic and blazing with holiness . . ."

In dissecting these verses, "putting your mind in gear" means to engage our sensory mind through the attention of our five senses on God. That's the only way we can be receptive to what Christ has for us. "Slipping back into the old grooves of evil, doing just what you feel like doing" is a specific reference to our old habits of thinking for ourselves. Our brain is a creature of habit and naturally feels like doing what it is used to doing all the time. When we don't choose to give God the attention of our five senses we will automatically return to our old "grooves"—our bad habit of thinking for ourselves.

In further breakdown of these verses from 1 Peter 1, "you didn't know any better then" are words written to encourage us not to beat ourselves up for our old habits of thinking for ourselves prior to being introduced to this new teaching of sensory focus on God. I never learned this teaching until the age of sixty, so I could really have a field day beating myself up for my many years of thinking for myself. Fortunately, continually devoting the attention of my five senses to God prevents me from beating myself up. If I even start to go down that road of self-abuse, those initial negative thoughts are my warning flag to get my sensory focus back on God. What an amazing sensory escape God gave me! He gave me a way out through heavenly addiction, "into a way of life shaped by God's life, a life energetic and blazing with holiness."

This ongoing sensory attention to God empties our minds of our own thoughts and leaves the thinking side of our brain open, like an empty vessel, waiting for his thoughts to pour into us. "A life energetic and blazing with holiness" is the miraculous outcome of giving the attention of our five senses to God so that he can fill our thinking mind with His thoughts. That is only possible when our five senses are focused on him and our thinking mind is empty of our own thoughts. In other words, our part is simply the choice to give God our sensory attention so he can take over our thought life. As a result, our thinking center becomes his domain, which allows him to perform in our lives and do all the work in our lives. He works in our lives through our thought domain, while we rest in him in our sensory domain. God designed our brains this way so he can fulfill his promise to direct our paths and run our lives.

This teaching has always been contained in God's word. I simply was not able to grasp it until I studied the brain and began reading his word with a whole new appetite for learning. The word "focus" became a central word in my vocabulary. I used to believe that focus meant trying hard to concentrate in my thought life. I tried to analyze and figure out everything, I worried about everything and the more I worried, the more my thoughts raced through my mind. I was a mental mess. Then, I tried even harder to think my way out of my mess. No wonder I came to the end of my rope and begged God to rescue me and take over my life! And wow, *how* he took over my life. Psalms 121:4-6 says that he "will never doze or sleep" (*The Message*)—he's on the job 24/7! I never imagined what an incredible job he would do running my life while I put my sensory focus on him.

At first, when I devoted my sensory focus on God, I was scared to death. I was at the end of my rope and started begging God to run my life, but I felt so afraid because I had never let anyone show me how to live every day. I was so fiercely independent that I felt totally helpless and fearful of what would happen to my life. Fortunately, God kept showing me scriptures multiple times a day that encouraged me and taught me how to go about this new life in him. Perhaps the most meaningful encouragement came from *The Message* in 1 Corinthians 2:2-5 where Paul says: "I was unsure of how to go about this, and felt totally inadequate—I was scared to death, if you want to know the truth of it—and so nothing I said could have impressed you or anyone else. But the message came through anyway. God's Spirit and God's power did it, which made it clear that your life of faith is a response to God's power, not to some fancy mental or emotional footwork by me or anyone else."

This scripture was so helpful to me, because even the incomparable Paul in the Bible experienced the same feelings I was having. Armed with this information, I embraced my inadequacy and trusted that God's Spirit and God's power were going to keep me on this new journey. As I focused on scriptures like this one, I slowly began to notice that my overwhelming fear was diminishing. Then God pointed me to another scripture that clearly explained *why* my fears and worry were subsiding. *The Message* in Philippians 4:6-7 says "Don't fret or worry. Instead of worrying, pray. Let petitions and praises shape your worries into prayers, letting God know your concerns. Before you know it, a sense of God's wholeness, everything coming together for good, will come and settle you down. It's wonderful what happens when Christ displaces worry at the center of your life."

That scripture was a real eye-opener for me. I always thought it was my job to stop my thoughts of worry. This scripture showed me that God takes away my worry when I focus on him by replacing worry with himself as the center of my attention. Once I began to see how God was starting to heal my worry and anxiety, I wanted to give him more and more go my sensory attention. Without fail, God showed me confirmation in scripture for my new desire. *The Message* in Luke 18:6-8 says ". . . So what makes you think God won't step in and work justice for his chosen people, who continue to cry out for help? Won't he stick up for them? I assure you, he will. He will not drag his feet. But how much of that kind of persistent faith will the son of man find on the earth when he returns?"

This scripture inspired me to continue to cry out for help by simply continuing to keep my sensory attention on God. It also inspired me to share and write about my new desire because of the challenge at the end of this verse: "But how much of that kind of persistent faith will the son of man find on the earth when he returns?" Never before did I experience a desire to share God with others. I only saw it as a responsibility or an obligation of my Christianity. This was so different! I wanted to tell everyone!

About the same time I was starting to get excited about sharing with others the new life God was pouring into me, I noticed another scripture that jumped off the page at me. *The Message* says in 2 Corinthians 1: 3-4 that "All praise to the God and Father of our Master, Jesus the Messiah! Father of all mercy! God of all healing counsel! He comes alongside us when we go through hard times, and before you know it, he brings us alongside someone else who is going through hard times so that we can be there for that person just as God was there for us." Incredible! God started bringing to me people that were longing for the same thing that I was thirsting for when I was at the end of my rope.

How quickly God showed me that sharing and writing was a fantastic way to maintain my sensory focus on him. Best of all, I was motivated to share and write without effort. God gave me everything to say and write which made me feel so special. God is able to treat each of us like we are his one and only child. I experienced how much God loved and cared for me because he gave me his constant attention. He lovingly and graciously filled me with his thoughts and words throughout each day. My only part was to continue to give him my sensory attention. God never stopped coming through for me in every way.

God continued to show me more and more scriptures about how to fix my five senses on him all day long. I learned that this sensory focus is a great working definition of "persistent faith" that I can grab onto. One of these scriptures about devoting my attention to God comes from Romans 12:1-2 where *The Message* says "So here's what I want you to do, God helping you: Take your everyday ordinary life—your sleeping, eating, going-to-work, and walking-around life—and place it before God as an offering. Embracing what God does for you is the best thing you can do for him. Don't become so well-adjusted to your culture that you fit into it without even thinking. Instead, fix your attention on God. You'll be changed from the inside out . . ."

This promise was irresistible to me. To learn that my sensory focus on God in every component of my daily life was an "offering" to him filled me with such unspeakable joy. I started to see that I was on the journey to becoming a heavenly addict. More and more, I was losing my self-inflicted need to focus on myself and to concentrate on my own negative thoughts and worries. When my old self decided to make guest appearances, I quickly used those unwanted appearances as a vivid reminder to run back into his arms. I began to see what the scriptures meant from *The Message* in Romans 8:12-14 where it says "So don't you see that we don't owe this old do-it-yourself life one red cent. There's nothing in it for us, nothing at all. The best thing to do is give it a decent burial and get on with your new life. God's Spirit beckons. There are things to do and places to go!"

Being in the moment with my five senses, paying attention to God and his surroundings and his loving presence in me has become an intense feeling I experience all the way deep into my bones. God continually floods my mind with his thoughts: Thoughts of instruction, revelation, praise, gratitude and thanksgiving. I can totally agree deep in my heart with Paul who writes in Romans 8:15-17 (*The Message*) that "This resurrection life you received from God is not a timid, grave-tending life. It's adventurously expectant, greeting God with a childlike 'What's next, Papa?' God's Spirit touches our spirits and confirms who we really are. We know who he is, and we know who we are: Father and children. And we know we are going to get what's coming to us—an unbelievable inheritance!"

"So if you're serious about living this new resurrection life with Christ, act like it. Pursue the things over which Christ presides. Don't shuffle along, eyes to the ground, absorbed with things right in front of you. Look up, and be alert to what is going on around Christ—that's where the action is. See things from his perspective" (Colossians 3:1-2, *The Message*).

Chapter Seven

Step-by-step: A FocusChoice Life

"Saving was all his idea, and all his work. All we do is trust him enough to let him do it. It's God's gift from start to finish! We don't play the major role. If we did, we'd probably go around bragging that we'd done the whole thing."

- Ephesians 2:8-9, *The Message*

Here are the five steps of FocusChoice Therapy, or what I have come to refer to as the FocusChoice Life equation or God's miracle prescription for emotional and spiritual health.

1. I choose sensory focus on God.
2. God floods my mind with thankful thoughts.
3. God fills my heart with his joy.
4 The joy of the Lord becomes my strength.
5. God displays his love in my life.

At first, many clients wonder about my use of the term "steps" in the FocusChoice Life equation, because these are not your typical performance steps. Performance steps specify something we have to do to achieve success. In our culture, steps are well known to require human effort and often times struggle on our part. These steps do not demand any effort on our part whatsoever. They do require action, however. The first action step is our choice to give the attention of our five senses to God. The remaining four steps are all about action on God's part—and fortunately we can always depend on him to complete his part in our lives.

As described in chapter six, sensory focus is a choice, which is the reason that I have named my new model for Christian Counseling "FocusChoice Therapy." The sensory focus on God described in chapter six constitutes step one of the FocusChoice life. This first step is the one and only step that God so graciously designed to be our part. He made sure that this first step only requires a sensory choice on our part, not a mental effort. In his infinite wisdom, God knew that requiring mental effort on our part would result in us taking our sensory focus off him and putting our attention back on ourselves. He wants us to totally depend on him to take over our lives. This requires that we permanently resign from the job of trying for ourselves and trying to run our own lives.

After step one, God takes responsibility for the rest of the steps on our behalf. These additional steps can be labeled from a healing perspective as God's divine medication. The second step that immediately follows the initial step of sensory focus (my working definition of faith), is God flooding our thinking minds with his thankful thoughts. He gives us a new dialect, as *The Message* says in Ephesians 5:4, ". . . Thanksgiving is our dialect."

Remember, there was no room for his thankful thoughts in our brain when our mental concentration was on our own efforts and worries. Now that our sensory focus is on God, we are free of our own negative thoughts and God bombards us with continual thoughts of thanksgiving. In *The Message*, Psalms 139: 17-18 says, "Your thoughts—how rare, how beautiful! God, I'll never comprehend them! I couldn't even begin to count them—any more than I could count the sand of the sea."

Many clients initially struggle with following step two. They try to make thanking God an effort on their part, rather than accepting that God fills the logical hemisphere of our brains with his thankful thoughts. I was working with a client recently who said it felt weird to thank God out loud for the beautiful breeze he enjoyed when he stepped outside into the cool morning air. The client said he knew he should thank God. I encouraged the client not to put pressure on himself with his "should" statements. I told him that simply choosing to allow himself to embrace and enjoy the nice breeze was step one. He was basking in the presence of God and remaining in his presence. He was enjoying his in-the-moment sensory experience with God.

Just because we don't give overt praise to God, it doesn't mean we are not appreciating our time with him. Sometimes, no words are even necessary. If we start thinking about what I should say to God, it moves our attention to the logical hemisphere of our brain and takes us out of our simple sensory indulgence in God. We have been erroneously taught by our culture and our churches to guilt ourselves, as if somehow we have taken God out of the picture. The truth is, since God is everywhere, our simple absence of words does not remove God from anything.

A second reason clients struggle with step two is because our culture and church have persistently taught us that action steps need to be measurable and progressive. They tend keep score of God's thoughts and put lots of effort into wondering if they have more or less of God's thoughts than others. They also try to hang onto the good feelings that follow any thoughts that God gives them as if God's thoughts are numbered and may run out.

That effort ends up ruining their feelings and they shame themselves for not achieving success. I ask clients if they struggle hanging onto the good feelings they experience during a nice glass of wine. They respond, of course not. They simply choose, without any mental effort, to enjoy another glass of wine. Our sensory focus on God is much like our indulgence in wine. The supply does not run out. However, unlike wine, where we get intoxicated and pass out after too much indulgence, we can become more and more intoxicated by God and never pass out.

What has amazed me most is how creative and constant God's thoughts are. Their flow is endless and beyond measurable. God readily gives us a fresh supply of his new thoughts every day. I see client after client all day long and God is constantly giving me new thoughts with words attached to share with my clients so I don't get insecure at the sound of my own voice or give up on myself. As *The Message* proclaims in 2 Corinthians 4:16-18 "So we're not giving up. How could we! Even though on the outside it often looks like things are falling apart on us, on the inside, where God is making new life, not a day goes by without his unfolding grace." I feel alive and filled with praise for him. He gives me such a release of natural pleasure chemicals and a supernatural high simply through filling my mind with his delightful thoughts.

This heavenly delight is something that I never experienced before in my life. In fact, I would make fun of others who seemed to find happiness in the relationship with God. Now, his wonderful thoughts loop back to the sensory side of my brain as God places his thoughts in me to make my five senses crave to stay in his presence. My five senses become even more eager to focus on him. My sight, sound, smell, taste and touch have developed such an acute sensitivity to focus on God. This love that he fills me with overflows into me feeling compassion and caring for others within my reach.

So, step two is God flooding my mind with thankful thoughts. In Colossians 3:17, *The Message* says: "Let every detail in your lives—words, actions, whatever—be done in the name of the Master, Jesus, thanking God the Father every step of the way." This instruction leads directly into step three, which is another step where God takes responsibility. He fills me over and over again with his joy. As a result of God implanting his thankful thoughts into my thinking brain, he fills my heart with joy.

This step is fundamental to the efficacy of FocusChoice Therapy. Most secular therapies are rooted in the cognitive or thinking side of our brain and feature the power of positive thinking and how it makes us feel good. These cognitive-based therapies are still immensely popular, but do not line up with what the Bible tells us or how God designed our brains.

From a Christian perspective, God filling us with his joy is what makes us feel good, not the power of positive thinking. If the power of positive thinking actually worked, no one would need God or need him to fill us with his joy. Making ourselves happy is impossible. Trying to overcome our negative thoughts with positive ones becomes a self-focused, futile endeavor. Our frustration with trying to replace our negative thoughts with positive ones simply reminds us of how bad we feel. Only God can make us feel better. He does this when we devote our sensory attention to him by giving us bountiful thoughts of thanksgiving, which fill our hearts with his joy.

The fourth step is what unfolds from God as he fills our hearts with his joy. The idea for step four originated with an ageless hymn entitled "The Joy of The Lord is My Strength." This is yet another step God fulfills on our behalf as we simply place our continual sensory focus on him. Our culture and even our churches attach the feeling of joy to how well we succeed or perform in life or in our Christian walk. In other words, we are taught that joy depends on our circumstances or how we measure up in handling those circumstances.

Far too many people have received false teaching from the church, instructing them to thank God for the hard times. God does not cause hard times. Mankind's poor choices and decisions cause hard times. Rather than thanking God for our hard times, we can thank him for staying in our presence and walking right beside us during hard times. "I'm absolutely convinced that nothing— nothing living or dead, angelic or demonic, today or tomorrow, high or low, thinkable or unthinkable— absolutely nothing can get between us and God's love because of the way that Jesus our Master has embraced us" (Romans 8:39, *The Message*).

Man's free will is at the root of bad things happening in our lives. Because God's master design for mankind included the dimension of free will, we simply cannot depend on God to make other people change. He invites them to change by giving their life to him, but only they can make the simple choice to let him run their lives. Their other choice is to continue to run their own lives. As long as people insist on running their own lives, those of us who have chosen to let God be in charge of our lives will experience hardships while still here on earth. *The Message* says in John 16:33 that "In this godless world you will continue to experience difficulties." Fortunately, God designed us with a way of escape to heavenly addiction so we can experience his joy regardless of having to endure the results of other people's poor choices. The ending of this verse from John 16:33 says "But take heart! I've conquered the world" (*The Message*). In other words, if we keep our focus on the conqueror, he will fill us with his joy despite any difficulties. In fact, he says, "I've told you all this so that trusting me, you will be unshakable and assured, deeply at peace" (John 16:32, *The Message*). Remember that the working definition of trusting God is giving him the attention of our five senses, instead of thinking about and dwelling on our circumstances.

God promises to carry us through both great times and miserable times, filled with his joy no matter what our circumstances, as long as we trust him through giving him our sensory focus. Maintaining our sensory focus on God can be compared to having a cord plugged into an electrical power source. The moment we take our eyes off him, we have unplugged and cut off our energy supply. We automatically put our focus back on ourselves and our circumstances. We have lost our power source.

As long as we remain unplugged we don't receive any power current or strength from God. As a result, we quickly get stuck on the emotional roller coaster ride of peaks and valleys that are part of the highs and lows of our self-centered existence here on earth. Fortunately, God formed our brain so that the roller coaster ride stops when we return our sensory attention to him. As soon as we plug in again with our sensory focus, his power current and energy supply once again to feed us his strength. We return to that stable, peaceful feeling that allows us to experience the joy God gives us.

A great sign that God is energizing us with his power and strength and bringing us his joy is the reaction we receive from those around us. They often see his energy and joy radiating from us even before we notice any changes in ourselves. His bright light shines in and through us so that others can see, but we are so focused on God and helping others that we are not noticing ourselves. Instead, we are putting our sensory focus on God and allowing him to do his work in and through us. We experience his joy even after a long day of God doing his work through our lives. We may feel physically tired and worn out, but emotionally and spiritually, we feel very joyful. We are thankful (not proud of ourselves) that God is using us for his glory and is sustaining us with his strength. We may even feel somewhat surprised when others notice how God is changing us because we have not been standing around taking selfies with our iPhone trying to show off how amazing we are. In fact, we feel tremendous relief that God is the amazing one—we no longer feel intense pressure to perform any work on our part.

God clearly shows us the distinction between his work and our work in *The Message* in Colossians 1:11-12 where the scripture says: "As you learn more and more how God works, you will learn how to do your work. We pray that you'll have the strength to stick it out over the long haul—not the grim strength of gritting your teeth but the glory-strength God gives. It is strength that endures the unendurable and spills over into joy, thanking the Father who makes us strong enough to take part in everything bright and beautiful that he has for us." These two verses are loaded with meaning. For years and years, my effort-based performance to serve God repeatedly resulted in mefeeling like a failure. Whatever strength I thought I generated through my own power certainly was grim. Now,

I feel reviewed to announce that I am and always will be a failure. I am okay with being a failure because I am now free to lean on Jesus. It is my keen sense of failure that propels me into his arms so I can be held up by his strength.

If you are starting to see that God's plan is so simple in terms of our "grim strength," you are correct. God made this plan simple on purpose because he doesn't want us to falsely believe that our efforts have anything to do with success in our relationship with him. God only requests that we make the simple choice to give him our continual sensory focus. God knows that, for the joy of the Lord to become our strength, our sensory focus needs to become sustained and not just happen once in a while. *The Message*, in Psalms 138:3 says "the moment I called out, you stepped in; you made my life large with strength." God fills us with strength the moment we call out, just like we smell the aroma of cookies the second we walk into the kitchen. The only way to catch the waves of "cookie aroma" is to stay in the kitchen. The only way to catch God's strength to the point so we can take part in "everything bright and beautiful that he has for us" is to stay in his kitchen, in his sensory presence.

Likewise, the only way to catch the rhythms or waves of his strength is to dwell with him on a continual basis and keep calling out to him. These rhythms or waves attached to each of our five senses are the mechanism that God created so we can continually call out to him and sustain our intimate attachment to him.

The Message in Matthew 11:29 tells us to "Learn the unforced rhythms of grace," which is like learning to dance with God. We watch all of God's movements, and as our dance teacher, he continually takes the lead and shows us how to move in unison and rhythm with him. It is this continual sensory attachment to God that builds our strength out of his joy.

To use my favorite example of the chocolate chip cookies yet again, it is the repetitive waves of their aroma that lift me up so high and make my desire for them so strong that I can no longer resist devouring them. In college, a couple of friends and I earned money in the summers by painting houses. One very sweet housewife baked us a huge batch of chocolate chip cookies and put them out in the farmhouse yard on the picnic table for the three of us painters to enjoy. We devoured them until not a single cookie was left. Needless to say, we all had stomach aches. Fortunately, when we devour God with our five senses, we don't become sick like we can with earthly addictions. His waves of joy overcome us and fill us with his strength, to the point where it generates spiritual electricity, turning us into his bright light. However, if we are constantly choosing to take our sensory focus off him, the electrical power cannot build to the level of a sustainable current that allow others to witness his light shining brightly in us.

The picture of his strength becoming a bright light in us as we sustain our sensory focus leads us to the fifth and culminating step that God performs in our lives. His strength that glows like a bright light displays his love in us. He is our only energy source for love. Philippians 2:13 says, "Be energetic in your life of salvation, reverent and sensitive before God. That energy is God's energy, an energy deep within you, God himself willing and working at what will give him the most pleasure" (*The Message*). God is the provider of both his love for us and our love for him and others. Loving ourselves or others on our own efforts is totally impossible. The harder we try, the more our love is self-centered. It comes across as self-serving to others and does not leave them feeling cared for or appreciated. No surprise there. From a FocusChoice perspective, human mental effort is by definition completely self-focus driven in its efforts to love.

When we give up on our human efforts to love and simply see ourselves as a conduit for God's love, we end up feeling such a freedom to love. This freedom to love grows as we get into rhythm with God. Matthew 11:30 immediately follows the "rhythms of grace" verse with "I won't lay anything heavy or ill-fitting on you. Keep company with me and you'll learn to live freely and lightly" (*The Message*). The more we dance with God and get into rhythm with him, the more we experience how he loves so unconditionally. We literally get into the flow of this love, which results in such total harmony and intimacy with God. This intimacy brings out even more thankfulness about his love for us. Remember that God implants his thankful thoughts in us, and those thoughts loop back to the sensory side of our brain and raise the intensity of each of our five senses to that heavenly addiction level. This heightened sensory awareness fills us with such love that we experience compassion and caring for those all around us.

What a different path to loving others than what we have previously been taught out of ignorance by our culture and church. We were taught that loving others was a responsibility we have as Christians, a responsibility to take the high road and perform loving actions, whether we felt loving or not. We were incorrectly taught that love was an action, not a feeling. We were incorrectly taught that love was a responsibility and requirement in our Christian walk. These false teachings only brought on guilt and shame for not being able to feel love for others like we were supposed to. What a relief to learn that love will just flow freely when we stop trying to love on our own and learn how to simply remain close to our Heavenly Father.

God's Word clearly says we are not capable of loving others in our own human strength. Others see right through our phony efforts and feel more unloved than ever. Only God can fill us with his love as the outcome of our sensory focus on him. Just like we use our five senses to pay attention to a person we are talking to, we can use our five senses to pay attention to God. Since God is all around us, and his Holy Spirit resides in us, we have his undivided attention all the time. He gives us this intimate attention as if we were his only child. In return, he desires our intimate, sensory attention. Through this sensory focus, we experience how deeply he loves us and he captures our love in return. In capturing our love, God gives us a heightened sensory awareness that shines through us as compassion and caring to others in our sphere of influence. Without any effort on our part, God gives us the gift of love, using us to truly bless others with his love, far beyond what we could ever imagine through trying to love on our own efforts.

This love that he implants deep within us is a powerful feeling that is emotionally turbo-charged and fresh and new every day. This love feels so good that we crave intimacy with God, just like an earthly addict craves to be with their addiction on a continual basis. Fortunately, unlike with earthly addictions, God's supply of love never runs out. We can totally rely on his love, whether we have a good or bad day. We can always depend on him to be our loving escape in a hostile, cut-throat world. His love invades our presence and we never have to chase him down to get his love and attention. As I just said, he makes us feel like his only child, even though he has millions of children around the globe. His love is addictive, and God intended it to be that way. No earthly addiction can even come close to measuring up to his love. Because he is the source of any love we feel, we are drawn to stay close to him. It is so nice to let go of our human drive to be independent. We start to thrive on our desire to cling to him. Even though that kind of utter dependency on anyone is frowned upon in our culture and church in today's world, we stop caring what the world says, and even what the religious crowd says. The more we maintain our sensory focus on God, dwelling in his loving embrace becomes our safe haven and refuge from what now feels like a foreign land here on earth.

"Christ will live in you as you open the door and invite him in. And I ask him that with both feet planted firmly on love, you'll be able to take in with all followers of Jesus the extravagant dimensions of Christ's love. Reach out and experience the breadth! Test its length! Plumb the depths! Rise to the heights! Live full lives, full in the fullness of God" (Ephesians 3:17-19, *The Message*).

Chapter 8

Sensory Dependence on God

"God, the one and only—
I'll wait as long as he says.
Everything I hope for comes from him,
so why not?
He's solid rock under my feet,
breathing room for my soul,
An impregnable castle:
I'm set for life.
My help and glory are in God
—granite-strength and safe-harbor-God—
So trust him absolutely, people;
lay your lives on the line for him.
God is a safe place to be."

- Psalm 62:5-8, *The Message*

Our church and culture devalue the word "dependency." We are all taught to be very proud of our independent spirit. Dependency on anything is considered a weakness. In the case of drug dependency, of course, everyone would agree that to be hooked on a drug is not good for us. But what about being hooked on God? Is that a good thing? What about sensory dependency on God? This kind of dependency is the answer of all answers. How do we become dependent on God with our five senses? My desire is that every reader will see how expansive, rather than small, sensory dependency on God is.

Our human nature is to try to put God in a box and specify certain universal activities as those that represent dependency on God, like praise and worship, Bible-reading, and prayer. The difficulty with qualifying these activities as God-dependent is the realization that any activity, including the traditional spiritual ones, are not automatically God-focused. Whether we are engaging in praise and worship, Bible-reading, prayer, or any spiritual activity, we can quite easily go through the motions without a genuine sensory focus or dependence on God with our five senses. For example, I can be singing verse after verse of a praise song while dwelling in my mind on a problem at work. It is not a particular action or activity that determines our sensory dependency on God, but how we engage with him through our five senses during every action or activity of our day.

Once we grasp the role of our five senses through understanding how God made our brains, we can give God our sensory attention throughout the day during all of our daily activities, whether we are at church, school, work, or our homes. Since God is continually in our presence with all his senses, it is completely up to us whether we will engage with him in sensory focus. Of course, God delights in us when we give him our total sensory attention, but he gives us the freedom to choose where we place the focus of our five senses. So many clients have honestly questioned their ability to become dependent and to make the continual choice to give their five senses to God. I always give clients who ask this question the same simple answer. We all have the ability to give any earthly passion our full sensory attention, so I am certain we have that same ability to give God our full sensory attention.

In the Bible, God spells out the notion of being in a close, continual relationship with him, so he definitely designed our brains with that capability. I have an earthly passion for baseball, so without any difficulty whatsoever, I can focus on baseball all day long and even at night when I sometimes wake up. At any time, day or night, I can always google my favorite team. Throughout the day and evening, I can watch the Little League World Series and any other level of baseball or softball on TV. Baseball can capture my sensory attention on a continual basis, because I love the sport so much.

My love affair with baseball started as a young boy when my father and brother would pitch to me with our barn doors as the backstop. I started buying bubblegum baseball cards for five cents a pack and began memorizing the player statistics. My love for baseball has never faded, but continually grown over the years, and even now I watch games every chance I get. With the advent of big screens, watching a game on television almost feels like being at the ball park.

For my whole life, I was taught by my church that I should be careful not to make baseball an idol in my life ahead of God. For many years, I've experienced a lot of shame because of this religious teaching. I felt like I must not love God as much as I should. But long after my baseball playing days had ended, God showed me that he is my biggest fan when it comes to baseball, whether I'm actually playing it or just watching the sport. God spoke to me gently about how much he enjoyed my love for baseball. He has continued to tell me how proud he is that I used the body and brain he created for me to play the game so well. He even tells me how proud he is as I continue to watch the sport as a hobby where I can relax and rest after a day of counseling others all day long. God has showed me that spending time enjoying baseball is a very wholesome way to relax and rest in him instead of being out a bar somewhere getting drunk to escape the pressures of life.

Just like God expressed in his Word, he is with me and all around me, and he is my partner in my passion for baseball. God entering into my love for baseball makes me feel so loved and cared for by God. I have learned that God is my true passion, and that baseball is simply one of my day-to-day activities that bind me to God and give me a heart of continual thanksgiving to God for how he takes care of me.

God desires to show all of us that he does not give us passions in a vacuum or without context. God will give every one of us who simply asks him an avenue or multiple avenues that make us able to continually maintain our sensory focus on him. One of the more recent avenues God has given me is writing books. He gave me this avenue to enjoy not as a job but as a means to continually uplift me. In any free moment God gives me, I love to write down what he shares with me. Sometimes, what God shares with me is a direct thought to me, but other times his thoughts come to me through another person or through the Bible or another resource. God's supply of these thoughts is endless. I am so dependent on them because the only other thought I have on my own anxious ones. I feel so much freedom for myself because the avenue of writing keeps my sensory focus continually on God.

God is always in "sensory time" with us. He is in a close, continual relationship with us, and never takes any of his attention off of us. However, I'm not trying to say that God loves everything we are thinking, saying, or doing at any given moment. Never in a million years would I say that, because God will never take pleasure with us in any moment where we hurt ourselves or others. In other words, God cannot enjoy binging on donuts or alcohol or any other earthly pleasure that hurts us physically, emotionally, socially, mentally, or spiritually. While we partake, God is there with us because he is everywhere, but he is not having fun like we think we are. God also will never participate with us in any sensory enjoyment that hurts others, like having sex with someone else's spouse. It is impossible for God to enjoy a sensory connection like that with us. God feels so much pain we hurt ourselves or others because we are his precious children, and he cannot join in where we are taking pleasure in something that will hurt us and/or others.

In reality, when we engage our five senses in anything that hurts ourselves or others, this is the exact moment that we take our sensory attention off of God. We are not in sensory time with him in any way, shape, or form—even when our sensory activity is still only in the mental stage and has not yet taken over our actions. For example, *The Message* says in Matthew 5:28, "But don't think you've preserved your virtues simply by staying out of bed. Your heart can be corrupted by lust even quicker than your body. Those leering looks you think nobody sees—they also corrupt."

Because we can so quickly take our sensory focus off of God, he never takes his focus off us for even a split second for any reason. God is able to give every one of his children his undivided attention and sensory focus each moment of every day. He lives inside us in the moment, whether we have our five senses fixed on him or not. He loves us so much that he feels pain the minute we withdraw our sensory focus from him, because he knows we are in immediate danger. He desires to protect us in every way possible and wants to be immediately available to us the moment we give our sensory attention back to him.

So how do I know if my sensory focus is on God or not? For example, is my sensory focus on him when I sleep? Definitely, because God delights in my sleep as I rest the amazing person he made me to be. I love to sleep and enjoy this form of rest in him. Now, if I start looking at porn instead of sleeping, then God hurts, because the child he loves is hurting himself instead of sleeping. My five senses are definitely on the porn instead of God. On the other hand, if a husband and wife wake up and enjoy sexual pleasure together, they have their sensory focus on God as they enjoy their five senses in the extraordinary way God made man and woman to come together in sexual pleasure.

There is not some mystical answer to whether our sensory focus is on God or not. The Bible's instructions are very clear cut when it comes to our sensory focus. *The Message* spells out these instructions in Philippians 4:8, "Summing it all up friends, I'd say you'll do best by filling your minds and meditating on things true, noble, reputable, authentic, compelling, gracious—the best, not the worst; the beautiful, not the ugly; things to praise, not things to curse. Put into practice what you learned from me, what you heard and saw and realized. Do that, and God, who makes everything work together, will work you into his most excellent harmonies."

The instructions of "filling your minds and meditating" are not about the power of positive thinking. Rather, they are about sensory focus on these things. Meditating means becoming emotionally involved and allowing yourself to feel what God feels. Meditating is definitely a sensory experience, not an intellectual exercise.

Simply recall your feelings of falling in love. Whether at work or play, you meditate on your new lover. You give your lover your sensory attention, even when you are not physically together. You remember a touch or kiss or smile or embrace throughout your time apart, and you long to be together again. God is continually at that level of close, sensory connection with us and longs for us to be at that same level of close connection with him. Since God is everywhere, and also lives inside of each of us, we can simply choose to be in the moment with him. The sense of closeness we feel in these moments is even better than with an earthly lover. Sometimes when we desire closeness, our partner is preoccupied, but God is never preoccupied. He is always ready and longing for our sensory closeness. As *The Message* says in John 4:14, "how bold and free we then become in his presence, freely asking according to his will, sure that he's listening."

Just as inspiring as God always being in sensory time with us, God joins us when we are in sensory closeness with another one of his children. He is thrilled with our sensory closeness to our spouse and children. As our Heavenly Father, he loves seeing his children gathered together, sharing with each other and him. It doesn't even have to be at church gathering. There doesn't even have to be prayer, music, or Bible reading. It can be at the dining room table together as a family enjoying a wonderful Christmas dinner together. I used to love our backyard football games in Virginia Beach with my family and relatives after a traditional Thanksgiving meal together. Simply enjoying each other's companionship in a wholesome way is a delightful time for our Heavenly Father as he watches over his children.

What if a family who does not believe in God experiences a lot of sensory closeness together? Is that sensory attachment they have with each other also their connection to God? Absolutely not. Despite the fact that God created all of us and is everywhere, we have no sensory connection with him until we choose to acknowledge him as our Creator and Heavenly Father. *The Message* says in 1 John 4:3 that "everyone who refuses to confess faith in Jesus has nothing in common with God."

However, once we make this simple choice to believe in him, he gives us the capacity to attach to him with our five senses on a non-stop basis. On a practical level, that acknowledgment of him translates into a tender moment of thanking him for giving us a beautiful family to enjoy special time together. As we maintain our sensory focus on God, our tender moments of feeling thankful to him start to string together into a continual feeling of love and appreciation to our Heavenly Father for always taking care of us.

As our moments of feeling thankful to God start to merge together, we begin the sensory journey of living in harmony with our Maker. For me, this journey has become like having an invisible best friend. I know God is in sensory time with me constantly, so I can be in constant sensory contact with him. Unlike any close contact I have with an earthly partner, where they may put my contact with them on hold because they don't want to be interrupted with what they are doing, God never puts me on hold. God is the perfect partner in a relationship. He gives me continual sensory access to him and never turns away when I reach out to him. He is always there for me at any time when I reach out to him with my five senses. Even better, he considers all my sensory awareness as sensory connection with him as long as it is wholesome. That means I am typically involved in daily living activities while I maintain sensory dependence on God. I maintain this sensory dependence on him as my coping mechanism to get through my day without being stuck in anxious, negativistic thinking.

Sensory dependence on God has been my only reliable and successful coping strategy to deal with the frequent, ongoing struggles of everyday life. Like many others, I have tried many earthly dependencies to cope with everyday difficulties in life, but none have provided any lasting relief. So many of us have tried the many earthly sensory dependencies such as alcohol, drugs, food, porn, or gaming to survive and make it through everyday life, only to discover we end up with more struggles than ever before. In our hopeless state, we make a last-ditch choice to give God a chance. Our last-ditch choice turns out to be the most amazing decision we ever made in our lives.

Our choice to give God our sensory devotion results in a lasting, victorious, sensory dependency on a solution that can carry us through this life and eternity. This idea is repeatedly confirmed in God's Word. In *The Message*, Paul writes in Philippians 4:7 that "it's wonderful what happens when Christ displaces worry at the center of your life." Paul goes on to write in the same chapter in Philippians in verses 13-14 that he'd "found a recipe for being happy whether full or hungry, hands full or hands empty. Whatever I have, wherever I am, I can make it through anything in the one who makes me who I am."

The Message also says in John 16:24 that "your joy will be like a river overflowing its banks," then in Ephesians 2:7, "now God has us where he wants us, with all the time in this world and the next to shower grace and kindness upon us in Jesus Christ." These verses show how much God wants to take care of us and be close to us. Of course he does! Each of us are his creation, each of us constitute a unique invention that God loves and adores.

In Psalm 138:13-16, David writes, "Oh yes you shaped me first inside, then out; you formed me in my mother's womb. I thank you, High God—you're breathtaking! Body and soul, I am marvelously made! I worship in adoration—what a creation! You know me inside and out, you know every bone in my body; you know exactly how I was made, bit by bit, how I was sculpted from nothing into something. Like an open book, you watched me grow from conception to birth; all the stages of my life were spread out before you, the days of my life all prepared before I'd lived even one day" (*The Message*).

These verses clearly demonstrate why God would give each of us his undivided sensory focus throughout our entire lives. Look at the close, detailed attention God gave us from the moment we were conceived! *The Message* in Psalms 139:2-6 shows how this sensory attention from God continues through our lives. "I'm an open book to you; even from a distance, you know what I'm thinking. You know when I leave and when I get back; I'm never out of your sight. You know everything I'm going to say before I start the first sentence. I look behind me and you're there, then up ahead and you're there, too—your reassuring presence, coming and going. This is too much, too wonderful—I can't take it all in!"

Many of us live our lives as if our only hope is to look out for ourselves. We have been so stubbornly independent, when all of this time God has longed for our sensory dependency on him. Thankfully, God has not withdrawn his attention from us, even for a second, through all the years we have wasted wandering around on our own. Even at our lowest point, God is instantly ready for us when we finally reach out to him. *The Message* says in Ephesians 2:5-6 that "Instead, immense in mercy and with an incredible love, he embraces us. He took our sin-dead life and made us alive in Christ. He did this all on his own with no help from us! Then he picked us up and set us down in highest heaven in company with Jesus, our Messiah."

Since God is forever committed to our sensory dependency on him, we can rest assured that God will never give up on showing us ways to express this dependency on him. By surrounding us with his presence and being alive in us, the contextual possibilities are endless as far as avenues to express our total sensory devotion to God.

One primary avenue God continually gives to us is our human relationships. Since God created all of mankind, his deepest desire is that all of his precious children come to know and experience his love. God's passion is that not a single one of his children miss out on sensory dependence on him. *The Message* says in 1 Timothy 2:4-5 that "he wants not only us but everyone saved, you know, everyone to get to know the truth we've learned: that there's one God and only one, and one Priest-Mediator between God and us—Jesus, who offered himself in exchange for everyone held captive by sin, to set them all free."

Simply engaging in relationships with others while our sensory dependency is on God is one of his favorite methods for us to express our love for him. A great biblical example was the relationship between Paul and Timothy. Paul says in 1 Timothy 1:12-18 that "I'm so grateful to Christ Jesus for making me adequate to do this work. He went out on a limb, you know, in trusting me with this ministry. The only credentials I brought to it were invective and witch hunts and arrogance. But I was treated mercifully because I didn't know what I was doing—didn't know who

I was doing it against! Grace mixed with faith and love poured over me and into me. And all because of Jesus. Here's a word you can take to heart and depend on: Jesus Christ came into the world to save sinners. I'm proof— Public Sinner Number One—of someone who never could have made it apart from sheer mercy. And now he shows me off—evidence of his endless patience—to those who are right on the edge of trusting him forever. . . I'm passing this work on to you, my son Timothy" (*The Message).*

Paul's connection with Timothy was what we would label today as a mentor relationship. The beauty of this relationship was Paul continually showing Timothy everything about sensory dependency on God that he had been shown himself. God provides us with many opportunities to be in relationship with others, where we can share with them are sensory focus on God. This relationship avenue always keeps our sensory dependency fresh and foremost on our minds. These relationships can range from our spouses, children, parents, extended family, friends, neighbors, coworkers, and anyone else God brings into our sphere of influence. I used to be so fearful talking to others about God, even my closest family members and friends. I would worry what they would think of me if I brought the topic of God into the conversation. Now that I have a couple years under my belt of practicing sensory focus on God, I am not the least bit fearful of talking about God with anyone. I long to share my ongoing experience of sensory focus on God with anyone and everyone. Talking about God is no longer just a topic of conversation but a sharing of my personal experience with my closest friend.

Even better, no one gets turned off by my personal sharing. I had a client many years ago tell me during our initial session never to bring up God in our counseling together. Of course, I agreed to respect his wishes. He spent over ten years coming to see me on a regular basis and I made sure I never offended him by talking about God. One session, out of the blue, my client reported he was back in a close relationship with God. He said he had been saved as a preteen in a Baptist Church in Pittsburgh, but turned his back on God for many years because his parents divorced. I asked him why he came back to God. He told me that, although I never mentioned the word God to him, he somehow knew that God was my closest friend. To this day, several years after my client passed away, I still do not know how he could tell. However, I am so grateful that my sensory dependency on God somehow displayed itself to my client before he died.

Becoming sensory-dependent on God has transformed me and my relationships. I am no longer an anxious mess in my relationships; instead, I enjoy living in the moment with my five senses engaged. This makes a radical difference for any of us in our day-to-day relationships. Our sensory engagement allows us to focus on the other person and not be preoccupied with ourselves. We attach to them emotionally and feel happy just being with them. We show a strong interest in them as a person, which makes them feel wanted and cared for. We also show compassion for them when they are hurting, and help them in any way possible. It is clear that our sensory dependency on God not only brings us into a close, caring relationship with him, but also with each other.

The Bible places a strong emphasis on our relationship with others as an intricate part of our loving relationship with God. God initiates the unconditional loving process in each of us and desires that we pass this unconditional love around to everyone we form a relationship with. *The Message* says in Psalms 61:5 that "you've always taken me seriously, God, made me welcome among those who know and love you." And "His love is the wonder of the world . . . Love God, all you saints; God takes care of all those who stay close to him" (Psalms 31:21-23). Then finally, in Ephesians 3:17-19, Paul says, "Christ will live in you as you open the door and invite him in. And I ask him that with both feet planted firmly on love, you'll be able to take in with all followers of Jesus the extravagant dimensions of Christ's love. Reach out and experience the breadth! Test its length! Plumb the depths! Rise to the heights! Live full lives, full in the fullness of God."

Sensory dependency on God is contagious. Giving God the attention of our five senses is how we open the door of our heart, so we can become sensory-dependent on him. As we join with others who are opening their hearts as well, we collectively experience the vastness and extravagance of his love. Sharing with others our sensory dependence on God only enriches our love for him and each other. The verses below highlight words of sensory dependency on God, words like hunger, thirst, eyes open, drinking in, take a breath, my arms wave, I smack my lips, shout, and run and play:

"God—you're my God! I can't get enough of you! I worked up such a hunger and thirst for God, traveling

across dry and weary deserts. So here I am in the place of worship, eyes open, drinking in your strength and glory. In your generous love I am really living at last! My lips brim praise like fountains. I bless you every time I take a breath; my arms wave like banners of praise to you. I eat my fill of prime rib and gravy; I smack my lips. It's time to shout praises! If I'm sleepless at midnight, I spend hours in grateful reflection. Because you've always stood up for me, I'm free to run and play. I hold on to you for dear life, and you hold me steady as a post. " (Psalm 63:1-8, *The Message*).

Chapter Nine

Intravenous Divine Medication

"He puts a little of Heaven in our hearts so that we'll never settle for less . . . Christ's love has moved me to such extremes. His love has the first and last word in everything we do."

- 2 Corinthians 5:5, 14, *The Message*

From working in drug treatment centers for fifteen years in the 1980's and 90's, I recall many drug addict stories where the user couldn't handle all the liquid drug from the needle. They became incredibly frustrated and anxious over wasting the extra drugs. If we were to picture God's divine prescription for joy as a liquid drug, we could say that when God injects his divine needle and feeds us his love intravenously, his love is often too much for us. We can't take it all in. However, there is no need for us to be anxious about losing out on what is left in the syringe, because his supply is continuous and the needle never needs to be pulled out of our veins.

Earthly medications can never measure up to God's supernatural love drug. All forms of illegal drug use have negative side effects, and due to elevating tolerance, addicts need more and more of the drug to have the same effect. God's love, on the other hand, is always sufficient and at maximum dosage, yet there is never any risk of overdosing. Plus, you don't need a new prescription for refills! God's prescription lasts forever and is always 100% effective. There are no generics or cheaper versions of his love. There is no fee to pick up his prescription, there are no insurance deductibles, and no waiting in line at the counter. Our body never becomes resistant or intolerant to God's love drug so that we have to discontinue our medication or switch to a new drug.

Perhaps the best news of all is that we can share his medication with our family and friends and anyone we want to without getting in trouble for dealing drugs. We don't have to worry about anyone being underage or even too old to take his medication safely. Dealing his divine medication by sharing God's love out of the abundance of his love for us becomes a primary way for us to keep our sensory focus on God. Sharing his love is the feedback loop that brings us back to our sensory focus on him. Sharing God's love with others is definitely a sensory-focus activity as we maintain eye contact, gently touch, and softly speak to others. As we maintain our sensory focus on God by sharing our feeling of intense love directly back to him in praise and thanksgiving, we are filled to overflowing with compassion for ourselves and with generosity and kindness to others.

This heavenly addiction that God gives us is totally free with no hidden costs, and it lasts forever because of the huge price he paid once and for all with his agonizing death on the cross at Calvary. Unlike earthly addictions, which traps us in a cycle of disease without cure, heavenly addiction is a radical cure for everyone who embraces God and the five steps of sensory focus on him. Sensory focus is the healing mechanism God designed to release our brains from earthly addictions.

When we simply turn our sensory focus to God, repetitively, day in and day out, God uses the same mechanism of sensory focus we used to become earthly addicts to retrain our brains to become heavenly addicts. Through repetitive sensory focus on God all the time, he heals our brain from earthly addictions and gives us more and more desire to focus on him. Our brain is a creature of habit and loves doing what it is used to focusing on. Our brain is just as capable of falling in love with God as it was capable of falling in love with earthly addictions. Until now, we have never been taught that sensory focus is the healing mechanism that transfers our brain's love affair from earthly to heavenly addictions.

There is no such word as "relapse" in heavenly addiction language, because God offers an eternal guarantee in exchange for our simple choice to give him our continual sensory focus. This guarantee is perhaps best expressed in *The Message* in Romans 8:29-30, where Paul writes: "God knew what he was doing from the very beginning. He decided from the outset to shape the lives of those who love him along the same lines as the life of his Son . . . After God made that decision of what his children should be like, he followed it up by calling people by name. After he called them by name, he set them up on a solid basis with himself. And then, after getting them established, he stayed with them to the end, gloriously completing what he had begun."

In FocusChoice Therapy terminology, these verses speak volumes about God's heavenly guarantee for our lives. The phrase, "those who love him" simply refers to those of us who devote the attention of our five senses to him. When we make that simple choice to make a sensory connection with God, he promises to shape our lives so that we look like his beloved son, Jesus. What a commitment on God's part to love us the same as he loves his own son—he even calls us by name! He adopts us into his primary family, promising to stay with us forever and complete his glorious work. Once we are closely attached to God and in his family, he gives us so much revelation into how to live our daily lives that we can totally depend on him to stick with us and take us all the way to the finish line.

Of course, we all slip and take our sensory focus off God many times a day. Unlike slips in earthly addiction, which are considered relapses, slips in heavenly addiction simply constitute reminders to quickly place our sensory focus back on God. Slips in earthly addiction lead back to active abuse. Slips in heavenly addiction simply lead back to focus on him. We get so addicted to God that we can't stand to be apart from him.

Our sensory dependency on God is beautifully described in Psalm 63:1-8, "God—you're my God! I can't get enough of you! I've worked up such hunger and thirst for God, traveling across dry and weary deserts. So here I am in the place of worship, eyes open, drinking in your strength and glory. In your generous love I am really living at last! My lips brim praises like fountains. I bless you every time I take a breath; my arms wave like banners of praise to you. I eat my fill of prime rib and gravy; I smack my lips. It's time to shout praises! If I'm sleepless at midnight, I spend the hours in quiet reflection. Because you've always stood up for me, I'm free to run and play. I hold on to you for dear life, and you hold me steady as a post" (*The Message*).

Just like there are earthly addiction cycles, there is a heavenly addiction cycle, where the more we give him our sensory focus, the more we fall in love with him. The more we fall in love with him, the more we desire to focus on him. Similarly, in an earthly addiction cycle, food for example, the more we focus on food, the more we want to eat the food that has the attention of our five senses. The more we eat this food, the more our desire for this food grows, which only intensifies our sensory attention to this food.

Any addiction can most accurately be described as an intense, sensory love affair. The problem is that every earthly addiction, however intense, is only a temporary love affair. The love turns to hate once the earthy addiction starts showing its ugly down-side; like in food addiction where we get obese. The great news about heavenly addiction is that it is a permanent and eternal love affair. There is never any down side or negative side effects, not in the short term, and not in the long term.

In earthly addictions, we never seem to run out of new ideas on how to get high. In heavenly addiction, God becomes the author of infinite, new ideas. He never shuts up with his creative and brilliant ideas for sharing his love to build our desire to sustain our sensory focus on him. He shows us so many ways to share his love back to him, including marveling at his mountains and valleys, skies and seas, flowers and trees, even sunshine and rain. We express his love to ourselves through exercise and nutrition, rest and play, even art and music. Since God created us, taking care of the bodies and minds he gave us is a great way to focus on him. Finally, we show his love to others through kind and caring words, acts of service and gifts and especially giving our time and attention to others.

Encouraging us to be his messengers and errand runners who share his love with others is perhaps God's most fascinating way of keeping our sensory attention on him. *The Message* in 2 Corinthians 1:4 says: "He comes alongside us when we go through hard times, and before you know it, he brings us alongside someone else who is going through hard times so that we can be there for that person just as God was there for us." When we share God's love with others as a way to maintain our sensory focus on him, "God leads us from place to place in one perpetual victory parade. Through us, he brings knowledge of Christ. Everywhere we go, people breathe in the exquisite fragrance. Because of Christ, we give off a sweet scent rising to God" (2 Corinthians 2:14-15, *The Message*). Others "suddenly recognize that God is a living, personal presence in us, not a piece of chiseled stone . . . Nothing between us and God, our faces shining with the brightness of his face. And so we are transfigured much like the Messiah, our lives gradually becoming brighter and more beautiful as God enters our lives and we become like him" (2 Corinthians 3:17-18, *The Message*).

In his genius, God ensures that others will not be misguided to only look at us and end up missing his brightness in us. If others did look at only us, we would be prone to putting our sensory focus back on ourselves rather than keeping our sensory attention on God. *The Message* says in 2 Corinthians 4:7-10 that, "We carry this precious Message around in unadorned clay pots of our ordinary lives. That's to prevent anyone from confusing God's incomparable power with us. As it is, there is not much chance of that. You know for yourselves that we're not much to look at. We've been surrounded and battered by troubles, but we're not demoralized; we're not sure what to do, but we know God knows what to do; we've been spiritually terrorized, but God hasn't left our side; we've been thrown down, but we haven't broken." 2 Corinthians 4 also goes on to say in verses 16-17 that "we're not giving up. How could we! Even though on the outside it often looks like things are falling apart on us, on the inside, where God is making new life, not a day goes by without his unfolding grace" (*The Message*).

In his grace, God never lets us out of his sight. He is always so close to us so that all we have to do is simply choose to give him the attention of our sight, sound, smell, touch and taste. He does all the work. He surrounds us with endless options of how to use those five senses from horseback riding on the beach to a quiet little cabin on the side of a mountain, or even a soft bath with nice candles burning.

Not all ways of using our five senses lead us to focus on God. One client whose spouse caught him looking at porn late at night explained to me that the porn helped him to relax after a long and trying day at work. While it is true that porn is easy to focus on as a sensory way to relax, it is not one of God's ideas on how to relax. However, when my client and his spouse started spending time together at night by having tea, they began to experience the benefits of engaging in God's ways for relaxation. On some nights, the relaxing from drinking tea even progressed to wanting to make love, which is a beautiful way that God created for couples to be sensory with each other.

One of my favorite examples of how to live a FocusChoice Life takes me back to my experience playing tennis. I consider tennis a great way for me to spend sensory time with God. I am enjoying the gifts he gave me of sensory focus and a sound body. I love playing sports and tennis is a great way for me to get physical exercise and to practice my sensory focus steps. Tennis is also a great way to relax and show God how much I love him by taking care of the mind and body he designed for me. I no longer fixate my thoughts on winning, which usually got in the way of winning anyway. I simply enjoy living in the sensory moment and experiencing my visual focus on the ball. Watching the ball instead of obsessing about winning has dramatically altered my game both in terms of speed and accuracy. I really enjoy this sensory success, yet feel no pressure to win and feel no anger when I lose. For me, tennis is *being*, not doing. Tennis is a work God is doing in me, and I am just enjoying the journey and the results God is achieving in me.

In his daily devotional book, "It Is Finished" Tullian Tchividjian writes for his February 26th entry about long distance athletes who run just for fun, rather than for a prize. These runners have been described as having "uncoupled performance from identity," a phrase which Tchividijian says "should hang over the door of every church and be emblazoned on the bathroom mirror of every Christian" (Tchividjian, 2015). In Philippians 4:1-4 says "If you've gotten anything out of following Christ, if his love has made any difference in your life, if being in a community of the Spirit means anything to you, if you have a heart, if you care—then do me a favor: Agree with each other, be deep-spirited friends. Don't push your way to the front; don't sweet-talk your way to the top. Put yourself aside, and help others get ahead. Don't be obsessed with getting your own advantage. Forget yourselves long enough to lend a helping hand" (*The Message)*.

I wholeheartedly agree with Tchividijian and with what Paul writes in Philippians 2. However, the question remains, how do we put ourselves aside—how do we uncouple performance from identity? My answer, as always, is the same: through giving God the attention of our five senses, which replaces our self-obsession. We don't perform the uncoupling, and God doesn't expect us to. God uncouples my performance from identity through my effortless choice to give him my sensory focus while he does all the rest. While I am focusing on him, God disconnects my performance from identity by him performing in me and giving me a new identity, his identity in me. He transforms me into his likeness and gives me the freedom to live in his reality.

Without a doubt, sensory focus on God goes well beyond the game of tennis or running or other ways to relax and exercise. In addition to the more well-known ways of focusing on God through reading his word, singing songs, and praying by ourselves or with other people, God has given us endless other sensory ways to share in an intimate relationship with him. Better than anyone, God understands that we have to go to work and school and study and do daily chores. He provides background sensory-focus ideas through all sorts of sights, sounds, smells, taste and touch to help us relax while we work and perform our daily tasks in life. We have headsets for background music, chairs to rock back and forth while we work and study, waterfalls and other nature sounds to plug in while we go about our business in our offices. God's background sensory distractions take away our anxiety while we need to concentrate on our work and study and chores. If we are performing mindless work or chores, these background sensory distractions keep our brains from being pulled back into anxious thinking. God has ideas to occupy the sensory side of our brain all day long, enabling us to continually remain in that close bond with him. He can even help us with something as small as chewing gum to satisfy our oral fix instead of eating too much and gaining weight.

One client in my counseling practice who is getting into the flow of sensory focus shared two very encouraging ways that he enjoys special moments with God. First, he shared that when he has his five senses on God and his mind is empty of his own "figuring-out problems" thinking, God graciously gives him a flurry of "pop in" thoughts that frequently solve the problem on his behalf. Second, while driving around on busy urban roads, he is always thanking God for his random acts of kindness, such as breaks in traffic and red lights staying green.

God know exactly how to fulfill his promise of "not letting a day go by without his unfolding grace" when he says in 1 John 4:19, "We, though, are going to love—love and be loved. First we were loved, now we love" (*The Message*). Basically, God promises to deliver an unconditional, loving, intimate relationship with us as a result of us taking one simple step of faith to put our sensory focus on him. That one simple choice is step one— and sensory focus on our part activates his promise which he always delivers through steps 2-4. God delivers in such a way that ". . . absolutely nothing can get between us and God's love because of the way Jesus our Master has embraced us." (Romans 8:39, *The Message*)

I vividly remember how my inpatient substance abuse clients would share their fantasies with me about a drug that would keep them high all the time. There is no earthly drug that comes even close to that fantasy. However, God actually delivers us into a heavenly addiction here on earth that is the ultimate high. *The Message* says in Ephesians 3:20 that "God can do anything you know—far more than you could ever imagine or guess or request in your wildest dreams! He does it not by pushing us around but by working within us, his Spirit deeply and gently within us." God does exactly that. He delivers new and creative thoughts and ideas every day that keep us high on him. He builds us up continually with his love, which is a constant encouragement to stay the course of keeping our five senses totally immersed on him. Now that is an addiction worth choosing!

Earthly addictions have as their final outcome a strong dependency that totally enslaves us. Heavenly addiction also has an outcome of utter dependency. However, total dependency on our all-knowing, ever-loving God does not enslave us, but sets us free. *The Message* says in Ephesians 1:7-9 that "Because of the sacrifice of the Messiah, his blood poured out on the altar of the Cross, we're a free people—free of penalties and punishments chalked up by all our misdeeds. And not just barely free, either, abundantly free! He thought of everything, provided for everything we could possibly need, letting us in on the plans he took such delight in making."

This abundant freedom from the penalties and punishments chalked up by all our misdeeds includes freedom from the emotional penalty of shame. When we are trapped in our earthly addictions, we are continually wearing a cloak of shame. As heavenly addicts, we no longer need to hang our heads in shame as we relate to God and others. We are free to live in intimacy, we can live in the moment engaged in a sensory way, and we can feel love and a caring connection in our relationships. As we experience life and relationships in the present, we are free from the distraction of dwelling on our past failures and shameful deeds.

The Message speaks about this freedom of heavenly addiction in Romans 8:1-2: "With the arrival of Jesus, the Messiah, that fateful dilemma is resolved. Those who enter into Christ's being-here-for-us no longer have to live under a continuous low-lying black cloud. A new power is in operation. The spirit of life in Christ, like a strong wind, has magnificently cleared the air, freeing you from a fated lifetime of brutal tyranny at the hands of sin and death."

This whole concept of heavenly addiction is not a far-out, New Age phenomenon. It is ageless and goes back before the beginning of time. Just prior to what *The Message* says in Ephesians 1:7-9, it says that God's plan for abundant freedom through heavenly addiction was formed long before he even created the earth. Verses 3-6 spell out this Master Plan: "How blessed is God! And what a blessing he is! He's the Father our Master, Jesus Christ, and takes us to the high places of blessing in him. Long before he laid down earth's foundations, he had us in mind, and settled on us as the focus of his love, to be made whole and holy by his love. Long, long ago he decided to adopt us into his family through Jesus Christ. (What pleasure he took in planning this!) He wanted us to enter into the celebration of his lavish gift-giving by the hand of his beloved Son."

"Keep your eyes on Jesus, who both began and finished this race we're in. Study how he did it. Because he never lost sight of where he was headed—that exhilarating finish in and with God—he could put up with anything along the way: Cross, shame, whatever. And now he's there, in the place of honor, right alongside God. When you find yourselves flagging in your faith, go over that story again, item by item, that long litany of hostility he plowed through. That will shoot adrenaline into your souls!" (Hebrews 12:2-3, *The Message*).

Chapter Ten

Living in God's Reality

"My dear children, let's not just talk about love; let's practice real love. This is the only way we'll know we're living truly, living in God's reality. It's also the way to shut down debilitating self-criticism, even when there is something to it. For God is greater than our worried hearts and knows more about us than we do ourselves."

- 1 John 3:18-20, *The Message*

Over the years, I have spent a lot of time imagining what God must experience in his relationship with me and all of his other children around the world. My only point of reference for my imagination is my relationship with my own two daughters. When they are hurting or in danger, I struggling emotionally as well—I can hardly stand it! What must it be like to live in God's shoes and live in his reality, where he never takes his sensory focus off any of his children? What unconditional love he shows us! He cares for each of us completely, continuously giving us the undivided attention of his five senses.

Of course, God also desires that we give him the undivided attention of our five senses on a constant basis, but rarely have any of us given God this level of sensory devotion. God desperately longs for us to live in his reality, with our five senses glued to him. Living in his reality at this deep, connected level is the only way we can depend on God so he can mold and shape us into his likeness. It is

God's only means to love us, protect us, and care for us in the intimate manner that he desires.

Plus, God depends on at least some of us to stay very close to him so that we can help round up all of his little ones that have wandered off the focus path. God pleads for us to join him in this continual roundup. He is not willing that any should perish or fall by the wayside. God will never rest because he is forever committed to all of us joining his family and living in his reality.

Dr. Rod Stafford, a pastor of Fairfax Community Church in Virginia, recently gave a sermon that perfectly illustrates what it means to live in God's reality (Stafford, 2015). In this message, Dr. Stafford speaks about living in God's reality by remembering that we have a home where we are never, never alone, and where we are invited to live as God's children, "living in the Spirit in His presence every day." Dr. Stafford emphasizes that, despite structures intended to remind us that we are God's beloved children, we function like orphans, as if we had been separated from and abandoned by our true families at birth. We move through our lives with a sense of deep disconnectedness, instead of like "beloved children who have a father who loves and adores us beyond measure. (Stafford, 2015)"

Despite this natural instinctive feeling of abandonment, we have assurance from the Bible of a promise of home, a place where we can feel loved, valued, understood, and protected, and where we can rest and be encouraged and restored. Dr. Stafford references the scriptural passage which states, "yet to all who received him, to those who believed on his name, he gave the right to become children of God (John 1:12-13, New

International Version)," children to whom Jesus made the promise, "I will not leave you as orphans; I will come to you" (John 14:18, NIV).

Dr. Stafford also reminds us of the words of God, where he proclaims, "I will be a Father to you, and you will be my sons and daughters, 2 Corinthians 6:18, NIV)," and the words of the apostle John where he exclaims, "How great is the love the Father has lavished on us, that we should be called children of God!" (1 John 3:1, NIV). Dr. Stafford goes on to say that these verses clearly show us that "God had all the provisions to find our way back to him and for us to have a home as his beloved children" (Stafford, 2015). This journey back to God begins with a decision, a simple choice to follow God, and this journey continues with ongoing, conscious choices to live our daily lives as his children, instead of continuing to live as if we were still abandoned orphans.

Dr. Stafford also highlights the role of the Holy Spirit living in our hearts and continually reminding us to live our daily lives as his beloved children. He quotes Galatians 4:4-6, where the scripture says, "But when the time had fully come, God sent his Son . . . that we might receive the full rights of sons. [And] because you are sons, God sent the Spirit of his Son into our hearts, the Spirit who calls out, 'Abba, Father.' (NIV)" Stafford explains that "walking in the Spirit is accepting who you are in Christ and accepting that you have been adopted as his beloved child by a Father who adores you beyond measure" (Stafford, 2015).

Stafford presents a helpful list to serve as a personal inventory in any given moment or situation, to help us distinguish whether we are walking in the Spirit as one of God's adopted children or whether we are still living in the "spirit of orphanhood" (Stafford, 2015). When we are living in the Spirit of God, we feel:

- Known and loved
- Accepted for who you are
- Generous, growing in the grace of giving
- Wholly dependent on God
- Moving confidently into the future
- Forgiving and able to offer grace
- Able to receive grace
- Open, honest, and vulnerable
- Humble
- Brave

Stafford also presents a counterpart list for each of these signs, indicating that we are living like abandoned orphans, which include feeling:

- Isolated and alone
- Need to put on some mask
- Selfish with time and possessions
- Self-reliant and independent
- Indecisive, worried about the future
- Judgmental, withholding grace
- Ashamed of mistakes you have already confessed
- Always striving for approval
- Always trying to prove your worth
- Consumed by anxiety and fear

Like many people, I became a poser as a young child and started wearing masks. I felt very insecure and broken, because I was taught early on that I was unlovable. My poser personality followed me into adulthood, where I became a man with the insecure, broken child still locked inside. For many years, I tried so hard to conquer my poser image, only to discover that I was getting worse. I had so many advice-givers who would dare me to be myself, but to me it was humanly impossible.

Recently, a well-respected nightly news anchor was suspended from his channel for being a poser. Although his net worth amounted to millions of dollars, this prominent, successful journalist felt the need to hide who he was. Having worked with clients from many different demographics, I suspect that famous, wealthy people are no different than the rest of us. No matter how successful we may look, and despite any accomplishments we can claim, deep inside, we are all very insecure and will always feel inadequate. We find it impossible to be "real." As performance-driven, self-critical, achievement-oriented individuals, even though we may proclaim that we are daring to be ourselves, we somehow drift further and further from this destiny with every passing year. We are all posers.

As sad as that pronouncement sounds, the truth is that God never created us with the ability or dare to be ourselves. He created us to rely on him, and to be like him. It is humanly impossible to be authentically real when we are relying our own merits, because we all inherit insecurity and brokenness. We all end up posing as successful, competent, independent adults, because that is what the world expects of us, but the truth is we all have an injured, frightened child locked away somewhere inside us. Despite our best human efforts and the advice from those around us, we continually fail to fix ourselves.

The typical outcome of this broken, anxiety-filled existence is that we resort to earthly addictions in a desperate attempt to make our life just a little better. We escape to the same places and activities that many other posers go to until they feel no pain. *The Message* says in Ephesians 4:17-18 that people like this have "refused for so long to deal with God that they've lost touch not only with God but with reality itself. They can't think straight anymore. Feeling no pain, they let themselves go into sexual obsession, addicted to every sort of perversion."

God dares us to deal with him through devoting our five senses to him rather than escaping to earthly addictions. God dares us to follow him so he can produce amazing results in our lives that we were incapable of accomplishing on our own. He dares us to follow him and become addicted to him, instead of continually escaping to earthly addictions. The miracle of God's dare is that, unlike human dares, there is absolutely no risk that God will abandon us or forget his promise to rescue us from ourselves.

When we give God all the attention of our five senses, he gives us a lifetime guarantee never to quit his job of running our lives. He also fulfills his promise to set us free from earthly addictions and their fatal outcome. Our God desires that we live in his presence every day, allowing him to fully direct our lives. He also gives us specific steps on how he fulfills this new reality in our daily lives. It is such a relief to learn the good news that God knows more about us than we know about ourselves. It is also good news that we can depend on him to run our lives rather than depending on ourselves and our flawed, broken system of performance addiction. It is even better news that God clearly shows us how to depend on him and live in his reality. The sad news is that it seems like relatively few people have been taught to do this.

Since God has recently showed me how it works to completely depend on him and live in his reality, my whole life has dramatically changed and I feel so much desire to share with everyone what I have learned. I am not the anxious mess I used to be, and I feel such freedom living in his love.

I make no excuses for not letting God show me at an earlier age how to live in his reality. He clearly shows us the way in his word, but I was so focused on myself that I never searched the scriptures. I also never took the time to learn how God designed my brain. God was intentional in the way he created the brain, so we can keep our sensory focus on him while he does our thinking for us. For me, studying God's handiwork in designing the human brain was an absolute revelation, and it opened my eyes to the incredible plan God has for each of us to live in his reality. As I studied this teaching, the Bible came alive for me for the first time.

Until this new teaching begins to capture the attention of hurting individuals everywhere, people will continue to only know of God from the thinking the side of their brain and will not experience his love on the sensory side of their brain. We all have basic human needs to feel loved and cared for, which are as fundamental as our human needs for food water and shelter. Without feeling the constant nourishment of God's love, we can experience emotional malnutrition and sensory deprivation, which leave us thirsting to death for earthly addictions.

When we only think about God and do not experience him deep in our hearts, it's no wonder that we end up desiring earthly addictions more than we desire God. However, if we just give God's plan a chance and put our sensory focus on our Father, he will show us that he is way more desirable and fascinating than any earthly addiction. As the *The Message* says in 2 Corinthians 5:5: "he puts a little heaven in our hearts so that we'll never settle for less."

God's promise to those of us who make the simple choice to devote our sensory attention to him includes some incredible gifts. *The Message* in Galatians 5:22-23 describes these gifts: "…affection for others, exuberance about life, serenity. We develop a willingness to stick to things. A sense of compassion in the heart, and a conviction that a basic holiness permeates things and people. We find ourselves involved in loyal commitments, not needing to force our way in life, able to marshal and direct our energies wisely."

Even better, living in God's reality through heavenly addiction to him here on earth is just a taste of our heaven to come! His love instills our longing for heaven, for eternity, deep in our hearts, so that we never again want to settle for the cheap, earthly, substitute addictions. No addiction or indulgence will ever satisfy this deep passion in our hearts for something beyond our own reality. Our true home, the place where we really belong, is with God.

His love, the wonder of this world, will be an even greater wonder in heaven.

I finally was open to God showing me that it is actually a good thing to be high on him and his love for me. God actually designed my brain to release pleasure chemicals to sustain me in his love. Learning that God designed my brain to get high through sensory focus on him has been the highlight of my relationship with God. What I learned about my brain was so instrumental in showing me the difference between *knowing* God and *experiencing* God. It showed me the difference between the simple choice to focus my five senses on him, versus my futile efforts to perform for him. It also showed me how it is possible to continually remain in God's presence at a sensory level without feeling pressure to think or act "religious" all the time.

By God showing me how to devote my sensory attention to him, he revealed to me the working definitions of faith, trust, and surrender, as well as walking in the spirit. God instructs me to have faith in him by looking up at him with my five senses, instead of putting my attention on myself and the mess that is right in front of me. This instruction reminds me of the "trust-walk" game, where we have blindfolds on our eyes and we allow someone to lead us around and trust them not to run us into a tree. Just think about this—our whole life can become a trust-walk with God! We have no idea what our future holds, but we allow him to continually lead us around by the hand, trusting that he knows where the next step will take us.

In other words, faith, trust, surrender, and walking in the spirit are not one-time decisions but continual moment-by-moment choices to put our sensory focus on God. Our only part in our relationship with God is to choose to keep our five senses focused on him. Amazingly, God made our brains so that this simple choice to be utterly dependent on him activates his performance in our lives. God doesn't even want us to think for ourselves. He knows it just makes us worry and be self-critical. God wants to think for us, make all the decisions in our lives and make every move on our behalf.

When we simply give God our sensory domain, he is able to invade our thought domain and run our lives on our behalf. Sensory focus is simply putting our faith in action by putting our faith in God to govern our lives as he sees fit. Because our culture and church have programmed us to run our own lives, putting our faith in God does not come naturally. That's why it is so brilliant that God made putting our faith in him through sensory focus such a simple, ongoing choice. Only God knew that we could never think our way into putting our faith in him. He knew we would credit ourselves if we were able to accomplish that feat. So he made it as simple as smelling the colorful flowers or watching the sunset or listening to the rhythmic chirping of the birds in the early morning hours. He designed our brains with a sensory half that requires no effort at all to have faith in him. It requires only the simple choice to give him our sensory focus. He does all the rest—he makes it so simple to live in his reality!

In the Old Testament times, it took the Israelites forty years of living in the wilderness and wandering around in circles year after year as they tried to get into the Promised Land through their own performance efforts.

Their forty years of futility was designed as an eleven-week journey if only they had kept their focus on God's direction. Fortunately, God never took his eyes off them and never abandoned them in their futility. In fact, God did not give up and still encouraged them to enter the Promised Land. *The Message* says in Deuteronomy 31:6-8: "Be strong. Take courage. Don't be intimidated. Don't give them a second thought, because God, your God is striding ahead of you. He's right there with you. He won't let you down. He won't leave you. . . you will enter the land with this people, this land that God promised their ancestors that he'd give them. You will make them the proud possessors of it. God is striding ahead of you. Don't be intimidated. Don't worry."

For me and many others in today's modern day world, we wander around year after year stuck in our own performance mentality, using earthly addictions as our only distractions from our sick, human thinking. We miss God's teaching and his simple clear instructions on how to quickly reach his promised land of heavenly addiction. *The Message* in Psalm 107:4-9 describes the outcome of our human performance efforts: "Some of you wandered for years in the desert, looking but not finding a good place to live. . . Staggering and stumbling, on the brink of exhaustion. Then, in your desperate condition, you called out to God . . . He put your feet on a wonderful road that took you straight into a good place to live. So thank God for His marvelous love. . . He poured great draughts of water down parched throats; the starved and hungry got plenty to eat."

I readily admit that I spent sixty years in effort-based futility, as I tried over and over again to have a happy personal life. Then, in barely six weeks of devoted attention to the Bible and how God designed the brain, God showed me magnificent glimpses of his promise land of heavenly addiction. He clearly revealed to me the secret of sensory focus that was the missing ingredient in my entire life. Once I made the simple choice to give God the ongoing attention of my five senses, the journey to the promise land of an intimate, loving relationship with him developed at lightning speed. As I was meditating on this beautiful transformation, God reminded me of the story of David fighting the giant Goliath, where a single stone was all that was needed to kill the giant. Through the single stone of sensory focus, God has slain the giant of despair in my life.

Millions of people like me wander in the wilderness year after year and continue to resist making this simple choice of sensory focus on God. However, many of my clients eagerly embrace this teaching, because they come to see me already completely exhausted from anxious, negativistic thinking. In their total brokenness, they reach out to me and ask for help. They feel like they are holding themselves together with scotch tape and are simply unable pick themselves up off the ground anymore. They are desperate enough to ask if there is any hope left for them. I ask them to take that first step of admitting they are at the end of their rope and ask if they are willing to make the simple choice to put their sensory focus on God.

Many clients admit to me that they are terrified to try to feel hope again, because they believe that they cannot handle any more disappointment or failure. I assure them that to give their sensory focus to God does not demand that they try to be hopeful. I explain that the practice of giving God the attention of our five senses does not require any effort or achievement on our part. God simply asks us to surrender our will to him by giving him our whole heart—our entire sensory attention. Many Christian advice-givers have shared these words of surrender with people but have failed to show them the follow-up steps of exactly what surrender looks like and how it works.

The entire purpose of FocusChoice Therapy and my mission is to teach everyone who will listen how it works. What remains is for me to teach people everywhere what giving God the attention of our five senses looks like and how that sensory focus activates surrender and the five steps to living in the freedom of God's control and his reality. The beauty of these steps is that God does the performing. Their only "work" in FocusChoice Therapy is to watch God work in them.

The Message in Matthew 11:28-30 confirms my instructions to watch God work in our lives: "are you tired? Worn out? Burned out on religion? Come to me. Get away with me and you'll recover your life. I'll show you how to take a real rest. Walk with me and work with me—watch how I do it. Learn the unforced rhythms of grace. I won't lay anything heavy or ill-fitting on you. Keep company with me and you'll learn to live freely and lightly." This scripture is too good to pass up! Just by being in God's company through our sensory attention to him, we can watch as he changes us.

The word "therapy" in FocusChoice Therapy still means change. However, in FocusChoice Therapy, God does the changing, not us. Clients are so relieved to learn that with this new FocusChoice Therapy, there won't be even more pressure put on them by me (the therapist) to get them to change their own lives through their own efforts. The very reason they came for counseling in the first place is because they folded under the pressure to perform and couldn't handle it anymore.

I believe most of the people who resist making the simple choice to focus on God are skeptical because our culture and church have given them such a distorted picture of God and his role in our lives. Even though millions of people are an anxious mess and feel totally impotent to run their own lives, many of our churches and spiritual leaders are still not instructing people from scriptures like this one in *The Message* out of Romans 4:19-25, which says: "Abraham didn't focus on his own impotence and say, 'It's hopeless.' This hundred-year-old body could never father a child. Nor did he survey Sarah's decades of infertility and give up. He didn't tiptoe around God's promise asking cautiously, skeptical questions. He plunged into the promise and came up strong, ready for God, sure that God would make good on what he had said. That's why it is said, 'Abraham was declared fit before God by trusting God to set him right.' But, it's not just Abraham; it's also us! The same thing gets said about us when we embrace and believe the one who brought Jesus to life when the conditions were equally hopeless. The sacrificed Jesus made us fit for God, set us right with God."

Just like with Abraham, God asks us to stop fixating on our impotent performance in life. He urges us to stop surveying our past history—to stop obsessing about our miserable track record in life. Those mental exercises are not what make us fit for God. The sacrificed Jesus made us fit for God; and, our sustained sensory focus on him keeps us in shape and strong in God. Of course, fear, hurt, anger, and anxiety can be triggered in us at any time simply through life circumstances. As these sensory interruptions creep in and momentarily distract us, God simply desires that these interruptions only serve as red flags to draw our attention back to him. However, when we allow these interruptions to draw our attention away from him by focusing on them and dwelling on them, God's strength in us quickly goes down the drain.

Only a rapid return to sensory focus on God allows his strength to remain in us. Otherwise, his energy does us no good, and we return to trying to run our own lives. God wants to have an active role in all of our life. However, he can only be active when we "plunge" into God's arms and "embrace" him with all of our sensory focus. Just like Abraham, God longs to have this same active, redemptive role with every one of us in today's world. Only He can rescue us from ourselves and the miserable, anxious mess we have made of our lives.

God rescues us and delivers us into a new reality of living and breathing him, simply through inviting us to focus on him with our five senses. In Romans 8:5-7 (*The Message*) the scriptures say, "Those who think they can do it on their own end up obsessed with measuring their own moral muscle but never get around to experiencing it in real life. Those who trust God's action in them find that God's spirit is in them-living and breathing God! Obsession with self in these matters is a dead end; attention to God leads us out into the open, into a spacious free life. Focus on self is the opposite of focusing on God."

When we remain steadfast in our sensory focus on God, we die to self and our own thoughts and obsessions. This "death to self" empties our own thoughts and opens up the thinking side of our brain as fertile ground for God to carry out his work in our lives. He created our brains so he could plant his thoughts in our minds. His thoughts will yield a bountiful harvest of words and actions that honor him and bless many others.

There is so much personal freedom that is attached to our sensory focus on God. When we die to self through our sensory focus on him, we are no longer prisoners to our own thoughts and the mental bondage that accompanies any preoccupation with self.

Some people picture God's role as the big bad wolf in their lives who will pounce on them when they fail. They have been taught that God expects them to perform at a very high level in order to satisfy him. They live in shame and guilt for failing to achieve at a high level in their relationship with God. They hang onto this belief in spite of scripture that clearly says that God loves us unconditionally and that all our human efforts to please him are totally futile.

God doesn't want us to focus on ourselves or dwell on our miserable failures, and he isn't waiting around to gloat over how badly we have screwed up. Far from it! Because of Christ's death on the cross, which proved once and for all that God loves us beyond measure, we no longer need to hold our heads in shame and guilt when we mess up. Through accepting God's unconditional love, we have been made righteous, something we can never do on our own. God wants us to celebrate his righteousness in us, not moan and groan because we don't always live or act like we've been saved.

Again, God does not want us to dwell in our misery and to keep trying with our futile efforts. He suffers with us in that misery and cries over how we keep wandering around obsessing about our failures. His death on the cross set us free from our own mental prison. God desperately desires that we dwell in his joy with him. He only wants our failures to quickly remind us that we slipped back into self-focus so we can just as quickly choose to shift our focus back to him. God designed our brain to quickly shift our focus back to him by simply crossing the bridge back to the sensory side of our brain.

While many fear that God is the big, bad wolf waiting to pounce on them with every screw up, others see God in the role as the magic fairy who hides them from the big bad wolf. They expect God somehow to make those around them change so they can live in a magic kingdom, free from fear. They focus on prayers that beg God to change their boss, their spouse, their children or their parents. God clearly says in the scriptures that there is no magic fairy or magic kingdom. He says to expect very difficult times in this world, because he gave everyone freedom of choice to follow him or do their own thing. God knows that many choose to do their own thing which always results in disaster. He knows we can't handle this disaster. That is precisely why he offers to run our lives for us.

Many clients are very angry at God deep down, because they hate the big bad wolf and they have found out he is not the magic fairy. They resist turning their lives over to someone with whom they are secretly angry. Clients are shocked when I suggest they boldly share their anger with God, even though God knows how they secretly feel anyway. They are even more shocked when God welcomes their anger and shows them incredible compassion for all the years of hurt that was trapped underneath their anger. Once clients get down to the hurt, they become more than willing to reach out to God and start letting him run their lives. For many clients, sharing their anger with God is their first step of sensory focus on him.

"You yourselves are a case study of what he does. At some point you all had your backs turned to God, thinking rebellious thoughts of him, giving him trouble every chance you got. But now, by giving himself completely at the cross, actually dying for you, Christ brought you over to God's side and put your lives together, whole and holy in his presence. You don't walk away from a gift like that! You stay grounded and steady in that bond of trust, constantly tuned in to The Message—just this one. Every creature under Heaven gets this same Message. I, Paul, am messenger to this Message" (Colossians 1:21-23, *The Message*).

Paul is a testimony to this scripture in Colossians. As Saul, his back was turned to God. He certainly was thinking rebellious thoughts about God, giving him trouble every chance he got by killing Jews. What a radical transformation God made in Saul when he became Paul! Jesus brought Paul over to God's side and put his life back together. Paul stayed grounded in that bond of trust by constantly being tuned in and focused on God with his five senses. Paul never looked back to himself or his natural abilities. He continually let God handle all the details of his life.

To sum it all up, we all know there are millions of hurting people in the world. We also know that major evil exists in this world, because so many of these hurting people choose to go their own way and hurt others. But God says if we simply choose to focus on him, he will run our lives so we can navigate our way through this evil world under his protection. He shows us that without him, we will end up as an anxious, miserable mess—like I did. Even though I thank God every day for showing me his plan for my life, I know that many other people are still living the lie that self-navigation and performance addiction is their only option. My desire is that, through this book, God will clear their vision and show them how to give him the focus of their heart, so he can put their lives back together, too.

"This is my life work: helping people understand and respond to this Message. It came as a sheer gift to me, a real surprise, God handling all the details . . . God saw to it that I was equipped, but you can be sure that it had nothing to do with my natural abilities" (Ephesians 3:7-8, *The Message).*

References

Alison, James. (2013). *Jesus the forgiving victim: Listening for the unheard voice.* Glenview, IL: Doers Publishing.

Kaufmann, Gershen. (1996). *The psychology of shame: Theory and treatment of shame-based syndromes.* New York, NY: Springer Publishing Company, Inc.

Lancer, Darlene. (2012). *Shame: The core of addiction and codependency.* Retrieved from http://darlenelancer.com/blog/shame-addiction-and-codpendency

Leaf, Caroline. (2016). *Controlling your toxic thoughts.* Retrieved from http://drleaf.com/about/toxic-thoughts

Petry, Nancy. et. al. (2014). An international consensus for assessing internet gaming disorder using the new DSM-5 approach. *Addiction, 109*(9): 1399-406.

Segal, Jeanne & Jaffe, Jaelline. (2016). *Attachment and adult relationships.* Retrieved from http://www.helpguide.org/articles/relationships/attachment-and-adult-relationships.htm

Stafford, Rod. (2015, September 13). Welcome home. Retrieved from http://fairfaxvideos.com/sermons/welcomehome/part1

Thinking Business, The. (2016). *Habits.* Retrieved from http://www.thethinkingbusiness.com/habits

Tozer, A. W. (2014). *The pursuit of God.* Ichthus Publications.

Tullian Tchividjian. (2015). *It is finished: 365 days of good news.* Colorado Springs, CO: David C. Cook.

About the Author

David Heebner, LPC, has had a broad and successful career of more than thirty years working in the field of mental healthcare; from helping individual clients with clinical or behavioral addiction issues, to running treatment centers that aide people in recovering from addictions of all kinds. Currently, David manages his own private practice in Chantilly, Virginia, where he provides outpatient services to individuals, couples, parents, and children. In 2012, David began to develop the FocusChoice Therapy model, which draws on spiritual principles and neuroscientific discoveries to bring peace and freedom to people who live imprisoned by performance-based thinking. He is also the author of *Clear My Vision: A Year of Focus on Christ.*

Made in the USA
Middletown, DE
28 July 2016